ALSO BY MARY BUFFETT AND DAVID CLARK

Buffettology

The Buffettology Workbook

The New Buffettology

The Tao of Warren Buffett

WARREN BUFFETT

AND THE

INTERPRETATION OF
FINANCIAL STATEMENTS

*The Search for the Company
with a Durable Competitive Advantage*

MARY BUFFETT *and* DAVID CLARK

Scribner

NEW YORK   LONDON   TORONTO   SYDNEY

SCRIBNER
A Division of Simon & Schuster, Inc.
1230 Avenue of the Americas
New York, NY 10020

First Scribner hardcover edition October 2008

SCRIBNER and design are registered trademarks of
The Gale Group, Inc., used under license
by Simon & Schuster, Inc., the publisher of this work.

For information about special discounts for bulk purchases,
please contact Simon & Schuster Special Sales at
1-800-456-6798 or business@simonandschuster.com.

Designed by Kyoko Watanabe
Text set in Sabon

Manufactured in the United States of America

1   3   5   7   9   10   8   6   4   2

Library of Congress Cataloging-in-Publication Data is available.

ISBN-13: 978-1-4165-7318-0
ISBN-10: 1-4165-7318-6

In loving memory of Patti Hansen Clark

*Founder of the Phoenix Academy of Learning
in Omaha, where over two thousand children with
learning disabilities have learned to read.*

*To learn more about the Phoenix Academy of Learning
please go to www.phoenixacad.com.*

Contents

THE INCOME STATEMENT

THE CASH FLOW STATEMENT

VALUING THE COMPANY WITH A
DURABLE COMPETITIVE ADVANTAGE

WARREN BUFFETT

AND THE

INTERPRETATION OF
FINANCIAL STATEMENTS

INTRODUCTION

For twelve years, from 1981 to 1993, I was the daughter-in-law of Warren Buffett, the world's most successful investor and now its greatest philanthropist.

Shortly after I married Warren's son Peter, and long before most of the world outside Wall Street had ever heard of Warren, I visited their family home in Omaha. While there, I met a small group of devoted students of the master investor's wisdom who referred to themselves as Buffettologists. One of the most successful Buffettologists, David Clark, kept notebooks filled with Warren's wisdom on investing, which were meticulous and endlessly fascinating to read. His notebooks were the foundation upon which he and I later shaped the internationally best-selling investment books: *The Tao of Warren Buffett, Buffettology, The Buffettology Workbook,* and *The New Buffettology,* which are now published in seventeen languages, including Hebrew, Arabic, Chinese, and Russian.

After the tremendous success of *The Tao of Warren Buffett,* I met up with David in Omaha during the 2007 Berkshire Hathaway annual meeting, and over lunch we fell into a discussion on the history of investment analysis. David pointed out that investment analysis during the late nineteenth century and the early part of the twentieth century was focused primarily on determining a company's solvency and earning power for the purposes of bond analysis. And that Benjamin Graham, the dean of Wall Street and Warren's mentor, had adapted early bond analysis techniques to common stocks analysis.

But Graham never made the distinction between a company that held a long-term competitive advantage over its competitors and one that didn't. He was only interested in whether or not the company had sufficient earning power to get it out of the economic trouble that had sent its stock price spiraling downward. He wasn't interested in owning a position in a company for ten or twenty years. If it didn't move after two years, he was out of it. It's not like Graham missed the boat; he just didn't get on the one that would have made him, like Warren, the richest man in the world.

Warren, on the other hand, after starting his career with Graham, discovered the tremendous wealth-creating economics of a company that possessed a long-term competitive advantage over its competitors. Warren realized that the longer you held one of these fantastic businesses, the richer it made you. While Graham would have argued that these super businesses were all overpriced, Warren realized that he didn't have to wait for the stock market to serve up a bargain price, that even if he paid a fair price, he could still get superrich off of those businesses.

In the process of discovering the advantages of owning a business with a long-term competitive advantage, Warren developed a unique set of analytical tools to help identify these special kinds of businesses. Though rooted in the old school Grahamian language, his new way of looking at things enabled him to determine whether the company could survive its current problems. Warren's way also told him whether or not the company in question possessed a long-term competitive advantage that would make him superrich over the long run.

At the end of the lunch, I asked David if he thought it would be possible to create a small, easy-to-use guide to reading a company's financial statement, using the unique set of tools Warren had developed for uncovering these wonderfully profitable businesses.

I envisioned a straightforward and easy-to-understand book that would teach investors how to read a company's financial statement, to look for the same kinds of companies that Warren does. A book that not only would explain what a balance sheet and income statement are, but would point out what investors should look for if, like Warren, they are searching for a company that possesses a long-term competitive advantage.

David loved the idea, and within a month we were trading back and forth chapters of the book you now hold in your hands, *Warren Buffett and the Interpretation of Financial Statements.*

We hope this book will help you make the quantum leap that Warren made by enabling you to go beyond the old-school Grahamian valuation models and discover, as Warren did, the phenomenal long-term wealth-creating power of a company that possesses a durable competitive advantage over its competitors. In the process you'll free yourself from the costly manipulations of Wall Street and gain the opportunity to join the growing ranks of intelligent investors the world over who are becoming tremendously wealthy following in the footsteps of this legendary and masterful investor.

MARY BUFFETT
JULY 2008

"*You have to understand accounting and you have to understand the nuances of accounting. It's the language of business and it's an imperfect language, but unless you are willing to put in the effort to learn accounting—how to read and interpret financial statements—you really shouldn't select stocks yourself.*"

—WARREN BUFFETT

CHAPTER 1

TWO GREAT REVELATIONS THAT MADE WARREN THE RICHEST PERSON IN THE WORLD

In the mid-sixties Warren began to reexamine Benjamin Graham's investment strategies. In doing so he had two stunning revelations about what kinds of companies would make the best investments and the most money over the long run. As a direct result of these revelations he altered the Graham-based value investment strategy he had used up until that time and in the process created the greatest wealth-investment strategy the world has ever seen.

It is the purpose of this book to explore Warren's two revelations—

1. How do you identify an exceptional company with a durable competitive advantage?
2. How do you value a company with a durable competitive advantage?

—to explain how his unique strategy works, and how he uses financial statements to put his strategy into practice. A practice that has made him the richest man in the world.

CHAPTER 2

THE KIND OF BUSINESS
THAT WILL MAKE WARREN
SUPERRICH

To understand Warren's first great revelation we need to understand the nature of Wall Street and its major players. Though Wall Street provides many services to businesses, for the last 200 years it has also served as a large casino where gamblers, in the guise of speculators, place massive bets on the direction of stock prices.

In the early days some of these gamblers achieved great wealth and prominence. They became the colorful characters people loved reading about in the financial press. Big "Diamond" Jim Brady and Bernard Baruch are just a few who were drawn into the public eye as master investors of their era.

In modern times institutional investors—mutual funds, hedge funds, and investment trusts—have replaced the big-time speculators of old. Institutional investors "sell" themselves to the masses as highly skilled stock pickers, parading their yearly results as advertising bait for a shortsighted public eager to get rich quickly.

As a rule, stock speculators tend to be a skittish lot, buying on good news, then jumping out on bad news. If the stock doesn't make its move within a couple of months, they sell it and go looking for something else.

The best of this new generation of gamblers have developed complex computer programs that measure the velocity of how fast a stock price is either rising or falling. If a company's shares are rising fast enough, the computer buys in; if the stock price is falling fast enough, the computer sells out. Which creates a lot of jumping in and out of thousands of different stocks.

It is not uncommon for these computer investors to jump into a stock one day, then jump out the next. Hedge fund managers use this system and can make lots and lots of money for their clients. But there is a catch: They can also lose lots and lots of money for their clients. And when they lose money, those clients (if they have any money left) get up and leave, to go find a new stock picker to pick stocks for them.

Wall Street is littered with the stories of the rise and fall of hot and not-so-hot stock pickers.

This speculative buying and selling frenzy has been going on for a long, long time. One of the great buying frenzies of all times, in the 1920s, sent stock prices into the stratosphere.

But in 1929 came the Crash, sending stock prices spinning downward.

In the early 1930s an enterprising young analyst on Wall Street by the name of Benjamin Graham noticed that the vast majority of hotshot stock pickers on Wall Street didn't care at all about the long-term economics of the businesses that they were busy buying and selling. All they cared about was whether the stock prices, over the short run, were going up or down.

Graham also noticed that these hot stock pickers, while caught up in their speculative frenzy, would sometimes drive up the stock prices to ridiculous levels in relation to the long-term economic realities of the underlying businesses. He also realized that these same hotshots would sometimes send stock prices spiraling to insane lows that similarly ignored the businesses' long-term prospects. It was in these insane lows that Graham saw a fantastic opportunity to make money.

Graham reasoned that if he bought these "oversold businesses" at prices below their long-term intrinsic value, eventually the market would acknowledge its mistake and revalue them upward. Once they were revalued upward, he could sell them at a profit. This is the basis for what we know today as value investing. Graham was the father of it.

What we have to realize, however, is that Graham really didn't care about what kind of business he was buying. In his world every business had a price at which it was a bargain.

When he started practicing value investing back in the 1930s, he was focused on finding companies trading at less than half of what they held in cash. He called it "buying a dollar for 50 cents." He had other standards as well, such as never paying more than ten times a company's earnings and selling the stock if it was up 50%. If it didn't go up within two years, he would sell it anyway. Yes, his perspective was a bit longer than that of the Wall Street speculators, but in truth he had zero interest in where the company would be in ten years.

Warren learned value investing under Graham at Columbia University in the 1950s and then, right before Graham retired, he went to work for him as an analyst in Graham's Wall Street firm. While there Warren worked alongside famed value investor Walter Schloss, who helped school young Warren in the art of spotting undervalued situations by having him read the financial statements of thousands of companies.

After Graham retired, Warren returned to his native Omaha, where he had time to ponder Graham's methodology far from the madding crowd of Wall Street. During this period, he noticed a few things about his mentor's teachings that he found troubling.

The first thing was that not all of Graham's undervalued businesses were revalued upward; some actually went into bankruptcy. With every batch of winners also came quite a few losers, which greatly dampened overall performance. Graham tried to protect against this scenario by running a broadly diversified portfolio, sometimes containing a hundred or more companies. Graham also adopted a strategy of getting rid of any stock that didn't move up after two years. But at the end of the day, many of his "undervalued stocks" stayed undervalued.

Warren discovered that a handful of the companies he and Graham had purchased, then sold under Graham's 50% rule, continued to prosper year after year; in the process he saw these companies' stock prices soar far above where they had been when Graham unloaded them. It was as if they bought seats on a train ride to Easy Street but got off well before the train arrived at the station, because he had no insight as to where it was headed.

Warren decided that he could improve on the performance of his mentor by learning more about the business economics of these "superstars." So he started studying the financial statements of these companies from the perspective of what made them such fantastic long-term investments.

What Warren learned was that these "superstars" all benefited from some kind of competitive advantage that created monopoly-like economics, allowing them either to charge more or to sell more of their products. In the process, they made a ton more money than their competitors.

Warren also realized that if a company's competitive advantage could be maintained for a long period of time—if it was "durable"—then the underlying value of the business would continue to increase year after year. Given a continuing increase in the underlying value of the business, it made more sense for Warren to keep the investment as long as he could, giving him a greater opportunity to profit from the company's competitive advantage.

Warren also noticed that Wall Street—via the value investors or speculators, or a combination of both—would at some point in the future acknowledge the increase in the underlying value of the company and push its stock price upward. It was as if the company's durable competitive advantage made these business investments a self-fulfilling prophecy.

There was something else that Warren found even more financially magical. Because these businesses had such incredible business economics working in their favor, there was zero chance of them ever going into bankruptcy. This meant that the lower Wall Street speculators drove the price of the shares, the less risk Warren had of losing his money when he bought in. The lower stock price also meant a greater upside potential for gain. And the longer he held on to these positions, the more time he had to profit from these businesses' great underlying economics. This fact would make him tremendously wealthy once the stock market eventually acknowledged these companies' ongoing good fortune.

All of this was a complete upset of the Wall Street dictum that to maximize your gain you had to increase your underlying risk. Warren had found the Holy Grail of investments; he had found an investment where, as his risk diminished, his potential for gain increased.

To make things even easier, Warren realized that he no longer had to wait for Wall Street to serve up a bargain price. He could pay a fair price for one of these super businesses and still come out ahead, provided he held the investment long enough. And, adding icing to an already delicious cake, he realized that if he held the investment long-term, and he never sold it, he could effectively defer the capital gains tax out into the far distant future, allowing his investment to compound tax-free year after year as long as he held it.

Let's look at an example: In 1973 Warren invested $11 million in The Washington Post Company, a newspaper with durable competitive advantage, and he has remained married to this investment to this day. Over the thirty-five years he has held this investment, its worth has grown to an astronomical $1.4 billion. Invest $11 million and make $1.4 billion! Not too shabby, and the best part is that because Warren has never sold a single share, he still has yet to pay a dime of tax on any of his profits.

Graham, on the other hand, under his 50% rule, would have sold Warren's Washington Post investment back in 1976 for around $16 million and would have paid a capital gains tax of 39% on his profits. Worse yet, the hotshot stock pickers of Wall Street have probably owned this stock a thousand times in the last thirty-five years for gains of 10 or 20% here and there, and have paid taxes each time they sold it. But Warren milked it for a cool 12,460% return and still to this day hasn't paid a red cent in taxes on his $1.4 billion gain.

Warren has learned that time will make him superrich when he invests in a company that has a durable competitive advantage working in its favor.

CHAPTER 3

WHERE WARREN STARTS
HIS SEARCH FOR THE
EXCEPTIONAL COMPANY

Before we start looking for the company that will make us rich, which is a company with a durable competitive advantage, it helps if we know where to look. Warren has figured out that these super companies come in three basic business models: They sell either a unique product or a unique service, or they are the low-cost buyer and seller of a product or service that the public consistently needs.

Let's take a good look at each of them.

Selling a unique product: This is the world of Coca-Cola, Pepsi, Wrigley, Hershey, Budweiser, Coors, Kraft, *The Washington Post,* Procter & Gamble, and Philip Morris. Through the process of customer need and experience, and advertising promotion, the producers of these products have placed the stories of their products in our minds and in doing so have induced us to think of their products when we go to satisfy a need. Want to chew some gum? You think of Wrigley. Feel like having a cold beer after a hot day on the job? You think of Budweiser. And things do go better with Coke.

Warren likes to think of these companies as owning a piece of the consumer's mind, and when a company owns a piece of the consumer's mind, it never has to change its products, which, as you will find out, is a good thing. The company also gets to charge higher prices and sell more of its products, creating all kinds of wonderful economic events that show up on the company's financial statements.

Selling a unique service: This is the world of Moody's Corp., H&R Block Inc., American Express Co., The Service-Master Co., and Wells Fargo & Co. Like lawyers or doctors, these companies sell services that people need and are willing to pay for—but unlike lawyers and doctors, these companies are institutional specific as opposed to people specific. When you think of getting your taxes done you think of H&R Block, you don't think of Jack the guy at H&R Block who does your taxes. When Warren bought into Salomon Brothers, an investment bank (now part of Citigroup), which he later sold, he thought he was buying an institution. But when top talent started to leave the firm with the firm's biggest clients, he realized it was people specific. In people-specific firms workers can demand and get a large part of the firm's profits, which leaves a much smaller pot for the firm's owners/shareholders. And getting the smaller pot is not how investors get rich.

The economics of selling a unique service can be phenomenal. A company doesn't have to spend a lot of money on redesigning its products, nor does it have to spend a fortune building a production plant and warehousing its wares. Firms selling unique services that own a piece of the consumer's mind can produce better margins than firms selling products.

Being the low-cost buyer and seller of a product or service that the public has an ongoing need for: This is the world of Wal-Mart, Costco, Nebraska Furniture Mart, Borsheim's Jewelers, and the Burlington Northern Santa Fe Railway. Here, big margins are traded for volume, with the increase in volume more than making up for the decrease in margins. The key is to be both the low-cost buyer and the low-cost seller, which allows you to get your margins higher than your competitor's and still be the low-cost seller of a product or service. The story of being the best price in town becomes part of the consumer's story of where to shop. In Omaha, if you need a new stove for your home, you go the Nebraska Furniture Mart for the best selection and the best price. Want to ship your goods cross-country? The Burlington Northern Santa Fe Railway can give you the best deal for your money. Live in a small town and want the best selection with the best prices? You go to Wal-Mart.

It's that simple: Sell a unique product or service or be the low-cost buyer and seller of a product or service, and you get to cash in, year after year, just as though you broke the bank at Monte Carlo.

CHAPTER 4

DURABILITY IS WARREN'S
TICKET TO RICHES

Warren has learned that it is the "durability" of the competitive advantage that creates all the wealth. Coca-Cola has been selling the same product for the last 122 years, and chances are good that it will be selling the same product for the next 122 years.

It is this consistency in the product that creates consistency in the company's profits. If the company doesn't have to keep changing its product, it won't have to spend millions on research and development, nor will it have to spend billions retooling its plant to manufacture next year's model. So the money piles up in the company's coffers, which means that it doesn't have to carry a lot of debt, which means that it doesn't have to pay a lot in interest, which means that it ends up with lots of money to either expand its operations or buy back its stock, which will drive up earnings and the price of the company's stock—which makes shareholders richer.

So when Warren is looking at a company's financial statement, he is looking for consistency. Does it consistently have high gross margins? Does it consistently carry little or no debt? Does it consistently *not* have to spend large sums on research and development? Does it show consistent earnings? Does it show a consistent growth in earnings? It is this "consistency" that shows up on the financial statement that gives Warren notice of the "durability" of the company's competitive advantage.

The place that Warren goes to discover whether or not the company has a "durable" competitive advantage is its financial statements.

CHAPTER 5

FINANCIAL STATEMENT OVERVIEW: WHERE THE GOLD IS HIDDEN

Financial statements are where Warren mines for companies with the golden durable competitive advantage. It is the company's financial statements that tell him if he is looking at a mediocre business forever moored to poor results or a company that has a durable competitive advantage that is going to make him superrich.

Financial statements come in three distinct flavors:

First, there is the *Income Statement*: The income statement tells us how much money the company earned during a set period of time. The company's accountants traditionally generate income statements for shareholders to see for each three-month period during the fiscal year and for the whole fiscal year. Using the company's income statement, Warren can determine such things as the company's margins, its return equity, and, most important, the consistency and direction of its earnings. All of these factors are necessary in determining whether the company is benefiting from a durable competitive advantage.

The second flavor is the *Balance Sheet*: The balance sheet tells us how much money the company has in the bank and how much money it owes. Subtract the money owed from the money in the bank and we get the net worth of the company. A company can create a balance sheet for any given day of the year, which will show what it owns, what it owes, and its net worth for that particular day.

Traditionally, companies generate a balance sheet for shareholders to see at the end of each three-month period of time (called quarter) and at the end of the accounting or fiscal year. Warren has learned to use some of the entries on the balance sheet—such as the amount of cash the company has or the amount of long-term debt it carries—as indicators of the presence of a durable competitive advantage.

Third, there is the *Cash Flow Statement*: The cash flow statement tracks the cash that flows in and out of the business. The cash flow statement is good for seeing how much money the company is spending on capital improvements. It also tracks bond and stock sales and repurchases. A company will usually issue a cash flow statement along with its other financial statements.

In the chapters ahead we shall explore in detail the income statement, balance sheet, and cash flow statement entries and indicators that Warren uses to discover whether or not the company in question has a durable competitive advantage that will make him rich over the long run.

CHAPTER 6

WHERE WARREN GOES TO FIND
FINANCIAL INFORMATION

In the modern age of the Internet there are dozens of places where one can easily find a company's financial statements. The easiest access is through either MSN.com (http://money central.msn.com/investor/home.asp) or Yahoo's Finance web page (www.finance.yahoo.com).

We use both, but Microsoft Network's MSN.com has more detailed financial statements. To begin, find where you type in the symbol for the stock quotes on both sites, then type in the name of the company. Click it when it pops up, and both MSN and Yahoo! will take you to that company's stock quote page. On the left you'll find a heading called "Finance," under which are three hyperlinks that take you to the company's balance sheet, income statement, and cash flow. Above that, under the heading "SEC," is a hyperlink to documents filed with the U.S. Securities and Exchange Commission (SEC). All publicly traded companies must file quarterly financial statements with the SEC; these are known as 8Qs. Also filed with the SEC is a document called the 10K, which is the company's annual report. It contains the financial statements for the company's accounting or fiscal year. Warren has read thousands of 10Ks over the years, as they do the best job of reporting the numbers without all the fluff that can get stuffed into a shareholders' annual report.

For the hard-core investor Bloomberg.com offers the same services and a lot more, for a fee. But honestly, unless we are buying and selling bonds or currencies, we can get all the financial information we need to build a stock portfolio for free from MSN and Yahoo! And "free" financial information always makes us smile!

THE
INCOME STATEMENT

"You have to read a zillion corporate annual reports and their financial statements."

—WARREN BUFFETT

"Some men read Playboy. *I read annual reports."*

—WARREN BUFFETT

CHAPTER 7

WHERE WARREN STARTS:
THE INCOME STATEMENT

Income Statement

($ in millions)

Revenue	$10,000
Cost of Goods Sold	3,000
Gross Profit	7,000
Operating Expenses	
Selling, General & Admin.	2,100
Research & Development	1,000
Depreciation	700
Operating Profit	3,200
Interest Expense	200
Gain (Loss) Sale Assets	1,275
Other	225
Income Before Tax	1,500
Income Taxes Paid	525
Net Earnings	$975

In his search for the magic company with a durable competitive advantage, Warren always starts with the firm's income statement. Income statements tell the investor the results of the company's operations for a set period of time. Traditionally, they are reported for each three-month period and at the end of the year. Income statements are always labeled for the time period they cover—such as January 1, 2007, to December 31, 2007.

An income statement has three basic components: First, there is the revenue of the business. Then there is the firm's expenses, which are subtracted from the firm's revenue and tell us whether the company earned a profit or had a loss. Sounds simple, doesn't it? It is.

In the early days of stock analysis the leading analysts of the time, such as Warren's mentor Benjamin Graham, focused purely on whether or not the firm produced a profit, and gave little or no attention to the long-term viability of the source of the company's earnings. As we discussed earlier, Graham didn't care if the company was an exceptional business with great economics working in its favor or if it was one of the thousands of mediocre businesses struggling to get by. Graham would buy into a lousy business in a heartbeat if he thought he could get it cheaply enough.

Part of Warren's insight was to divide the world of businesses into two different groups: First, there were the companies that had a long-term durable competitive advantage over their competitors. These were the businesses which, if he could buy them at a fair or better price, would make him superrich if he held them long enough. The other group was all the mediocre businesses that struggled year after year in a competitive market, which made them poor long-term investments.

In Warren's search for one of these amazing businesses, he realized that the individual components of a company's income statement could tell him whether or not the company possessed the superwealth-creating, long-term durable competitive advantage that he so coveted. Not just whether or not the company made money. But what kind of margins it had, whether it needed to spend a lot on research and development to keep its competitive advantage alive, and whether it needed to use a lot of leverage to make money. These factors comprise the kind of information he mines from the income statement to learn the nature of a company's economic engine. To Warren, the source of the earnings is always more important than the earnings themselves.

For the next fifty chapters we are going to focus on the individual components of a company's financial statement and what Warren is searching for that will tell him if this is the kind of business that will send him into poverty, or the golden business with a long-term durable competitive advantage that will continue to make him one of the richest people in the world.

CHAPTER 8

REVENUE:

WHERE THE MONEY COMES IN

Income Statement	
($ in millions)	
→ Revenue	$10,000
Cost of Goods Sold	3,000
Gross Profit	$7,000

The first line on the income statement is always total, or gross, revenue. This is the amount of money that came in the door during the period of time in question, which is reported either quarterly or yearly. If we are manufacturing shoes and we sell $120 million worth of shoes in a year, we will report $120 million of total revenue for the year on our yearly income statement.

Now the fact that a company has a lot of revenue doesn't mean that it is earning a profit. To determine if a company is earning a profit, you need to deduct the expenses of the business from its total revenues. Total revenue minus expenses equals net earnings. But the total revenue number by itself tells us nothing until we subtract the expenses and find out what the net earnings are.

After Warren has taken a peek at the total revenues of a business, he starts a long and careful dig through the expenses. Because Warren knows that one of the great secrets to making more money is spending less money.

CHAPTER 9

Cost of Goods Sold:
For Warren the Lower the Better

Income Statement	
($ in millions)	
Revenue	$10,000
→ Cost of Goods Sold	3,000
Gross Profit	$7,000

On the income statement, right under the line for Total Revenue comes the Cost of Goods Sold, also known as the Cost of Revenue. The cost of goods sold is either the cost of purchasing the goods the company is reselling or the cost of the materials and labor used in manufacturing the products it is selling. "Cost of revenue" is usually used in place of "cost of goods sold" if the company is in the business of providing services rather than products. Essentially they are the same thing—but one is a little more encompassing than the other. We should always investigate exactly what the company is including in its calculation of its cost of sales or cost of revenue. This gives us a good idea of how management is thinking about the business.

A simple example of how a furniture company might calculate its cost of goods number would be: Start with the cost of the company's furniture inventory at the beginning of the year; add in the cost of adding to the furniture inventory during the year; and then subtract the cash value of the furniture inventory left at the end of the year. Therefore, if a company starts the year with $10 million in inventory, makes $2 million in purchases to add to the inventory, and ends the period with an inventory whose cost value is $7 million, the company's cost of goods for the period would be $5 million.

Although the cost of goods sold, as a lone number, doesn't tell us much about whether the company has a durable competitive advantage or not, it is essential in determining the Gross Profit of the business, which is a key number that helps Warren determine whether or not the company has a long-term competitive advantage. We discuss this further in the next chapter.

CHAPTER 10

GROSS PROFIT/GROSS PROFIT MARGIN: KEY NUMBERS FOR WARREN IN HIS SEARCH FOR LONG-TERM GOLD

Income Statement	
($ in millions)	
→ Revenue	$10,000
Cost of Goods Sold	3,000
→ Gross Profit	$7,000

Gross Profit $7,000 ÷ Revenue $10,000 = Gross Profit Margin 70%

Now if we subtract from the company's total revenue the amount reported as its Cost of Goods Sold, we get the company's reported Gross Profit. An example: total revenue of $10 million less cost of goods sold of $7 million equals a gross profit of $3 million.

Gross profit is how much money the company made off of total revenue after subtracting the costs of the raw goods and the labor used to make the goods. It doesn't include such categories as sales and administrative costs, depreciation, and the interest costs of running the business.

By itself, gross profit tells us very little, but we can use this number to calculate the company's gross profit margin, which can tell us a lot about the economic nature of the company.

The equation for determining gross profit margin is:

$$\text{Gross Profit} \div \text{Total Revenues} = \text{Gross Profit Margin}$$

Warren's perspective is to look for companies that have some kind of durable competitive advantage—businesses that he can profit from over the long run. What he has found is that companies that have excellent long-term economics working in their favor tend to have **consistently** higher gross profit margins than those that don't. Let me show you:

The gross profit margins of companies that Warren has already identified as having a durable competitive advantage include: Coca-Cola, which shows a consistent gross profit margin of 60% or better; the bond rating company Moody's, 73%; the Burlington Northern Santa Fe Railway, 61%; and the very chewable Wrigley Co., 51%.

Contrast these excellent businesses with several companies we know that have poor long-term economics, such as the in-and-out-of-bankruptcy United Airlines, which shows a gross profit margin of 14%; troubled auto maker General Motors, which comes in at a weak 21%; the once troubled, but now profitable U.S. Steel, at a not-so-strong 17%; and Goodyear Tire—which runs in any weather, but in a bad economy is stuck at a not-very-impressive 20%.

In the tech world—a field Warren stays away from because he doesn't understand it—Microsoft shows a consistent gross profit margin of 79%, while Apple Inc. comes in at 33%. These percentages indicate that Microsoft produces better economics selling operating systems and software than Apple does selling hardware and services.

What creates a high gross profit margin is the company's durable competitive advantage, which allows it the freedom to price the products and services it sells well in excess of its cost of goods sold. Without a competitive advantage, companies have to compete by lowering the price of the product or service they are selling. That drop, of course, lowers their profit margins and therefore their profitability.

As a very general rule (and there are exceptions): Companies with gross profit margins of 40% or better tend to be companies with some sort of durable competitive advantage. Companies with gross profit margins below 40% tend to be companies in highly competitive industries, where competition is hurting overall profit margins (there are exceptions here, too). Any gross profit margin of 20% and below is usually a good indicator of a fiercely competitive industry, where no one company can create a sustainable competitive advantage over the competition. And a company in a fiercely competitive industry, without some kind of competitive advantage working in its favor, is never going to make us rich over the long run.

While the gross profit margin test is not fail-safe, it is one of the early indicators that the company in question has some kind of consistent durable competitive advantage. Warren strongly emphasizes the word "durable," and to be on the safe side we should track the annual gross profit margins for the last ten years to ensure that the "consistency" is there. Warren knows that when we look for companies with a durable competitive advantage, "consistency" is the name of the game.

Now there are a number of ways that a company with a high gross profit margin can go astray and be stripped of its long-term competitive advantage. One of these is high research costs, another is high selling and administrative costs, and a third is high interest costs on debt. Any one of these three costs can destroy the long-term economics of the business. These are called operating expenses, and they are the thorn in the side of every business.

CHAPTER 11

OPERATING EXPENSES:
WHERE WARREN KEEPS A CAREFUL EYE

Income Statement	
($ in millions)	
Revenue	$10,000
Cost of Goods Sold	3,000
Gross Profit	7,000
→ Operating Expenses	
Selling, General & Admin.	2,100
Research & Development	1,000
Depreciation	700
Operating Profit	$3,200

Right beneath the line on the income statement for gross profit comes a group of expenses called operating expenses.

These are all the company's hard costs associated with research and development of new products, selling and administrative costs of getting the product to market, depreciation and amortization, restructuring and impairment charges, and the catch-all "other" that includes all non-operating, non-recurring expenses.

When these entries are added, they make up the company's total operating expenses, which are then subtracted from the gross profit to give us the firm's operating profit or loss. Since these entries all have an impact on the long-term economic nature of the business, it is best if we spend the next couple of chapters going through them one by one in true Warren fashion.

CHAPTER 12

SELLING, GENERAL, AND ADMINISTRATIVE EXPENSES

Income Statement	
($ in millions)	
Revenue	$10,000
Cost of Goods Sold	3,000
Gross Profit	7,000
Operating Expenses	
→ Selling, General & Admin.	2,100
Research & Development	1,000
Interest	700
Operating Profit	$3,200

On the income statement under the heading of Selling, General & Administrative (SGA) Expenses is where the company reports its costs for direct and indirect selling expenses and all general and administrative expenses incurred during the accounting period. These include management salaries, advertising, travel costs, legal fees, commissions, all payroll costs, and the like.

With a company like Coca-Cola, these expenses run into the billions and have a tremendous impact on the company's bottom line. As a percentage of gross profit, they vary greatly from business to business. They even vary with companies like Coca-Cola that have a durable competitive advantage. Coca-Cola consistently spends on average 59% of its gross profit on SGA expenses. A company like Moody's consistently spends on average 25%, and Procter & Gamble consistently spends right around 61%. "Consistently" is the key word.

Companies that don't have a durable competitive advantage suffer from intense competition and show wild variation in SGA costs as a percentage of gross profit. GM, over the last five years, has gone from spending 28% to 83% of its gross profits on SGA costs. Ford, over the last five years, has been spending 89% to 780% of its gross profits on SGA expenses, which means that they are losing money like crazy. What happens is that sales start to fall, which means revenues fall, but SGA costs remain. If the company can't cut SGA costs fast enough, they start eating into more and more of the company's gross profits.

In the search for a company with a durable competitive

advantage the lower the company's SGA expenses, the better. If they can stay consistently low, all the better. In the world of business anything under 30% is considered fantastic. However, there are a number of companies with a durable competitive advantage that have SGA expenses in the 30% to 80% range. But if we see a company that is repetitively showing SGA expenses close to, or in excess of, 100%, we are probably dealing with a company in a highly competitive industry where no one entity has a sustainable competitive advantage.

There are also companies with low to medium SGA expenses that destroy great long-term business economics with high research and development costs, capital expenditures, and/or interest expense on their debt load.

Intel is a perfect example of a company that has a low ratio of SGA expenses to gross profit, but that because of high research and development costs has seen its long-term economics reduced to just average. Yet if Intel stopped doing research and development, its current batch of products would be obsolete within ten years and it would have to go out of business.

Goodyear Tire has a 72% ratio of SGA expenses to gross profit, but its high capital expenditures and interest expense—from the debt used to finance its capital expenditures—are dragging the tire maker into the red every time there is a recession. But if Goodyear didn't add the debt to make all those capital expenditures/improvements, it wouldn't stay competitive for very long.

Warren has learned to steer clear of companies cursed with consistently high SGA expenses. He also knows that the economics of companies with low SGA expenses can be destroyed by expensive research and development costs, high capital expenditures, and/or lots of debt. He avoids these kinds of businesses regardless of the price, because he knows that their inherent long-term economics are so poor that even a low asking price for the stock will not save investors from a lifetime of mediocre results.

CHAPTER 13

RESEARCH AND DEVELOPMENT: WHY WARREN STAYS AWAY FROM IT

Income Statement	
($ in millions)	
Revenue	$10,000
Cost of Goods Sold	3,000
→ Gross Profit	7,000
Operating Expenses	
Selling, General & Admin.	2,100
→ Research & Development	1,000
Depreciation	700
Operating Profit	$3,200

$\mathbf{T}$his is a big one in the game of identifying companies with a durable competitive advantage. What seems like a long-term competitive advantage is often an advantage bestowed upon the company by a patent or some technological advancement. If the competitive advantage is created by a patent, as with the pharmaceutical companies, at some point in time that patent will expire and the company's competitive advantage will disappear.

If the competitive advantage is the result of some technological advancement, there is always the threat that newer technology will replace it. This is why Microsoft is so afraid of the technological advancements of Google. Today's competitive advantage may end up becoming tomorrow's obsolescence.

Not only must these companies spend huge sums of money on R&D, but because they are constantly having to invent new products they must also redesign and update their sales programs, which means that they also have to spend heavily on selling and administrative costs. Consider this: Merck must spend 29% of its gross profit on R&D and 49% of its gross profit on selling, general, and administrative costs (SGA), which, when combined, eat up a total 78% of its gross profit. What's more, if Merck & Co. fails to invent the next new multibillion-dollar-selling drug, it loses its competitive advantage when its existing patents expire.

Intel, while the leader in its fast-paced field, must consistently spend approximately 30% of its gross profit on R&D expenses; if it doesn't, it will lose its competitive advantage within just a few years.

Moody's, the bond rating company, is a long-time Warren favorite, with good reason. Moody's has no R&D expense, and on average spends only 25% of its gross profit on SGA expenses. Coca-Cola, which also has no R&D costs, but has to advertise like crazy, still, on average, spends only 59% of its gross profit on SGA costs. With Moody's and Coca-Cola, Warren doesn't have to lie awake at night worrying that some drug patent is going to expire or that his company won't win the race to the next technological breakthrough.

Here then is Warren's rule: Companies that have to spend heavily on R&D have an inherent flaw in their competitive advantage that will always put their long-term economics at risk, which means they are not a sure thing.

And if it is not a sure thing, Warren is not interested.

CHAPTER 14

DEPRECIATION:
A COST WARREN CAN'T IGNORE

Income Statement

($ in millions)

Revenue	$10,000
Cost of Goods Sold	3,000
→ Gross Profit	7,000
Operating Expenses	
Selling, General & Admin.	2,100
Research & Development	1,000
→ Depreciation	700
Operating Profit	$3,200

All machinery and buildings eventually wear out over time; this wearing out is recognized on the income statement as depreciation. Basically, the amount that something depreciates in a given year is a cost that is allocated against income for that year. This makes sense: The amount by which the asset depreciated can arguably be said to have been used in the company's business activity of the year that generated the income.

An example: Imagine that a million-dollar printing press is bought by XYZ Printing Corporation. This printing press has a life span of ten years. Because it has a life span of ten years, the Internal Revenue Service will not let the company expense the entire $1 million cost in the year that it was purchased. Instead, the press must be expensed over the ten years that it is in service. A ten-year life span and an original cost of $1 million will mean that XYZ will depreciate the printing press at a rate of $100,000 a year. Depreciation is a real cost of doing business, because at some time in the future, the printing press will have to be replaced.

The buying of the printing press will—on the balance sheet—cause $1 million to come out of cash and $1 million to be added to plant and equipment. Then, for the next ten years, the depreciated cost of $100,000 a year will show up on the income statement as an expense. On the balance sheet each year, $100,000 will be subtracted from the plant and equipment asset account and $100,000 added to the accumulated depreciation liability account. The actual $1 million cash outlay for the printing press will show up on the cash flow statement under capital expenditures. We would like to emphasize that the million-dollar expense for the printing press is not taken in the year that it is bought; rather it is allocated as a depreciation expense to the income statement, in $100,000 increments, over a ten-year period.

A neat trick that Wall Street financial types have figured out is that once the printing press is bought and paid for, the $100,000 yearly depreciation expense doesn't take any more additional cash outlays, but it does decrease earnings that are reported to the IRS every year for the next ten years. This means that, from a short-term perspective, XYZ has a yearly cost that in reality isn't costing it any additional outlays of cash. Thus, the Wall Street financial types can add that $100,000 cost back into earnings, which means that the cash flow of the business can now support more debt for such fun money-making ventures as leveraged buyouts. Wall Street has an acronym for this earnings recalculation: They call it EBITDA—meaning Earnings Before Income Tax, Depreciation, and Amortization.

Warren says that by using EBITDA our clever Wall Street types are ignoring that eventually the printing press will wear out and the company will have to come up with another $1 million to buy a new one. But now the company is saddled with a ton of debt left over from the leveraged buyout and might not have the ability to finance the $1 million purchase of a new printing press.

Warren believes that depreciation is a very real expense and should always be included in any calculation of earnings.

To do otherwise would be to delude ourselves over the short-term into believing that business is earning more than it actually is. And one does not get rich off delusions.

What Warren has discovered is that companies that have a durable competitive advantage tend to have lower depreciation costs as a percentage of gross profit than companies that have to suffer the woes of intense competition. As an example, Coca-Cola's depreciation expense consistently runs about 6% of its gross profits, and Wrigley's, another durable competitive advantage holder, also runs around 7%. And Procter & Gamble, another long-time Warren favorite, comes in at approximately 8%. Contrast the case of GM, which is in a highly competitive capital-intensive business. Its depreciation expense runs anywhere from 22% to 57% of its gross profits.

As with any expense that eats into a company's gross profits, Warren has found that less always means more—when it comes to increasing the bottom line.

CHAPTER 15

INTEREST EXPENSE:
WHAT WARREN DOESN'T WANT

Income Statement

($ in millions)

Revenue	$10,000
Cost of Goods Sold	3,000
→ Gross Profit	7,000
Operating Expenses	
Selling, General & Admin.	2,100
Research & Development	1,000
Depreciation	700
Operating Profit	3,200
→ Interest Expense	$200

Interest Expense is the entry for the interest paid out, during the quarter or year, on the debt the company carries on its balance sheet as a liability. While it is possible for a company to be earning more in interest than it is paying out, as with a bank, the vast majority of manufacturing and retail businesses pay out far more in interest than they earn.

This is called a financial cost, not an operating cost, and it is isolated out on its own, because it is not tied to any production or sales process. Instead, interest is reflective of the total debt that the company is carrying on its books. The more debt the company has, the more interest it has to pay.

Companies with high interest payments relative to operating income tend to be one of two types: a company that is in a fiercely competitive industry, where large capital expenditures are required for it to stay competitive, or a company with excellent business economics that acquired the debt when the company was bought in a leveraged buyout.

What Warren has figured out is that companies with a durable competitive advantage often carry little or no interest expense. Long-term competitive advantage holder Procter & Gamble has to pay a mere 8% of its operating income out in interest costs; the Wrigley Co. has to pay an average 7%; contrast those two companies with Goodyear, which is in the highly competitive and capital-intensive tire business. Goodyear has to pay, on average, 49% of its operating income out in interest payments.

Even in highly competitive businesses like the airline industry, the amount of the operating income paid out in interest can be used to identify companies with a competitive advantage. The consistently profitable Southwest Airlines pays just 9% of operating income in interest payments, while its in-and-out-of-bankruptcy competitor United Airlines pays 61% of its operating income out in interest payments. Southwest's other troubled competitor, American Airlines, pays a whopping 92% of its operating income out in interest payments.

As a rule, Warren's favorite durable competitive advantage holders in the consumer products category all have interest payouts of less than 15% of operating income. But be aware that the percentage of interest payments to operating income varies greatly from industry to industry. As an example: Wells Fargo, a bank in which Warren owns a 14% stake, pays out approximately 30% of its operating income in interest payments, which seems high compared with Coke's, but actually makes the bank, out of America's top five, the one with the lowest and most attractive ratio. Wells Fargo is also the only one with a AAA rating from Standard & Poor's.

The ratio of interest payments to operating income can also be very informative as to the level of economic danger that a company is in. Take the investment banking business, which on average makes interest payments in the neighborhood of 70% of its operating income. A careful eye would have picked up the fact that in 2006 Bear Stearns reported that it was paying out 70% of its operating income in interest payments, but that by the quarter that ended in November 2007, its percentage of interest payments to operating income had jumped to 230%. This means that it had to dip into its shareholders' equity to make up the difference. In a highly leveraged operation like Bear Stearns, that spelled disaster. By March of 2008 the once mighty Bear Stearns, whose shares had traded as high as $170 the year before, was being forced to merge with JP Morgan Chase & Co. for a mere $10 a share.

The rule here is real simple: In any given industry the company with the lowest ratio of interest payments to operating income is usually the company most likely to have the competitive advantage. In Warren's world, investing in the company with a durable competitive advantage is the only way to ensure that we are going to get rich over the long-term.

CHAPTER 16

GAIN (OR LOSS) ON
SALE OF ASSETS AND OTHER

Income Statement	
($ in millions)	
Operating Expenses	
Selling, General & Admin.	$2,100
Research & Development	1,000
Depreciation	700
Operating Profit	3,200
Interest Expense	200
→ Gain (Loss) Sale Assets	1,275
→ Other	225

When a company sells an asset (other than inventory), the profit or loss for the sale is recorded under Gain (or Loss) on

Sale of Assets. The profit is the difference between the proceeds from the sale and the carrying amount shown on the company's books. If the company had a building that it paid $1 million for, and after depreciating it down to $500,000, sold it for $800,000, the company would record a gain of $300,000 on the sale of the asset. Likewise, if the building sold for $400,000, the company would record a loss of $100,000.

The same thing applies to the entry "Other." This is where non-operating, unusual, and infrequent income and expense events are netted out and entered onto the income statement. Such events would include the sale of fixed assets, such as property, plant, and equipment. Also included under "Other" would be licensing agreements and the sale of patents, if they were categorized as outside the normal course of business.

Sometimes these nonrecurring events can significantly add to a company's bottom line. Since these *are* nonrecurring events, Warren believes that they should be removed from any calculation of the company's net earnings in determining whether or not the company has a durable competitive advantage.

CHAPTER 17

INCOME BEFORE TAX:
THE NUMBER THAT WARREN USES

Income Statement

($ in millions)

Operating Expenses	
Selling, General & Admin.	$2,100
Research & Development	1,000
Depreciation	700
Operating Profit	3,200
Interest Expense	200
Gain (Loss) Sale Assets	1,275
Other	225
→ Income Before Tax	$1,500

"Income before tax" is a company's income after all expenses have been deducted, but before income tax has been subtracted. It is also the number that Warren uses when he is calculating the return that he is getting when he buys a whole business, or when he buys a partial interest in a company through the open-market purchase of its shares.

With the exception of tax-free investments, all investment returns are marketed on a pre-tax basis. And since all investments compete with each other, it is easier to think about them if they are thought about in equal terms.

When Warren bought $139 million worth of tax-free bonds in Washington Public Power Supply System (WPPSS), which paid him $22.7 million a year in tax-free interest, he reasoned that an after-tax $22 million was the same as earning a pre-tax $45 million. To buy a business that would earn him a pre-tax $45 million would cost him $250 million to $300 million. Thus, he viewed the WPPSS bonds as a business that he was buying at a 50% discount, relative to the value of what other businesses with similar economics were selling for.

Warren has always discussed the earnings of a company in pre-tax terms. This enables him to think about a business or investment in terms relative to other investments. It is also one of the cornerstones of his revelation that a company with a durable competitive advantage is actually a kind of "equity bond," with an expanding coupon or interest rate. We shall explore his "equity bond" theory in much greater detail toward the end of the book.

CHAPTER 18

INCOME TAXES PAID:
HOW WARREN KNOWS WHO
IS TELLING THE TRUTH

Income Statement	
($ in millions)	
Operating Expenses	
Selling, General & Admin.	$2,100
Research & Development	1,000
Depreciation	700
Operating Profit	3,200
Interest Expense	200
Gain (Loss) Sale Assets	1,275
Other	225
Income Before Tax	1,500
→ Income Taxes Paid	$525

Just like every other taxpayer, American corporations have to pay taxes on their income. Today, in America, that amount is approximately 35% of their income. When taxes are paid, they are recorded on the income statement under the heading Income Taxes Paid.

Now what is interesting about Income Taxes Paid is that the line item reflects the company's true pre-tax earnings. Sometimes, companies like to tell the world that they are making more money than they actually are. (Shocking, isn't it?) One of the ways to see if they are telling the truth is to look at the documents they file with the SEC and see what they are paying in income taxes. Take the number they list as pre-tax operating income and deduct 35% from it. If the remainder doesn't equal the amount the company reported as income taxes paid, we had better start asking some questions.

Warren has learned over the years that companies that are busy misleading the IRS are usually hard at work misleading their shareholders as well. The beauty of a company with a long-term competitive advantage is that it makes so much money it doesn't have to mislead anyone to look good.

CHAPTER 19

NET EARNINGS:
WHAT WARREN IS LOOKING FOR

Income Statement	
($ in millions)	
Operating Expenses	
Selling, General & Admin.	$2,100
Research & Development	1,000
Depreciation	700
Operating Profit	3,200
Interest Expense	200
Gain (Loss) Sale Assets	1, 275
Other	225
Income Before Tax	1,500
Income Taxes Paid	525
→ Net Earnings	$975

After all the expenses and taxes have been deducted from a company's revenue, we get the company's net earnings. This is where we find out how much money the company made after it paid income taxes. There are a couple of concepts that Warren uses when he looks at this number that help him determine whether the company has a durable competitive advantage, so why don't we start there.

First on Warren's list is whether or not the net earnings are showing a historical upward trend. A single year's entry for net earnings is worthless to Warren; he is interested in whether or not there is consistency in the earnings picture and whether the long-term trend is upward—both of which can be equated to "durability" of the competitive advantage. For Warren the ride doesn't have to be smooth, but he is after a historical upward trend.

But note: Because of share repurchase programs it is possible that a company's historical net earnings trend may be different from its historical per-share earnings trend. Share repurchase programs will increase per-share earnings by decreasing the number of shares outstanding. If a company reduces the number of shares outstanding, it will decrease the number of shares being used to divide the company's net earnings, which in turn increases per-share earnings even though actual net earnings haven't increased. In extreme examples the company's share repurchase program can even cause an increase in per-share earnings, while the company is experiencing an actual decrease in net earnings.

Though most financial analysis focuses on a company's

per-share earnings, Warren looks at the business's net earnings to see what is actually going on.

What he has learned is that companies with a durable competitive advantage will report a higher percentage of net earnings to total revenues than their competitors will. Warren has said that given the choice between owning a company that is earning $2 billion on $10 billion in total revenue, or a company earning $5 billion on $100 billion in total revenue, he would choose the company earning the $2 billion. This is because the company with $2 billion in net earnings is earning 20% on total revenues, while the company earning $5 billion is earning only 5% on total revenues.

So, while the total revenue number alone tells us very little about the economics of the business, its ratio to net earnings can tell us a lot about the economics of the business compared with other businesses.

A fantastic business like Coca-Cola earns 21% on total revenues, and the amazing Moody's earns 31%, which reflects these companies' superior underlying business economics. But a company like Southwest Airlines earns a meager 7%, which reflects the highly competitive nature of the airline business, in which no one airline holds a long-term competitive advantage over its peers. In contrast, General Motors, in even a great year—when it isn't losing money—earns only 3% on total revenue. This is indicative of the lousy economics inherent in the supercompetitive auto industry.

A simple rule (and there are exceptions) is that if a company is showing a net earnings history of more than 20% on total revenues, there is a real good chance that it is benefiting from some kind of long-term competitive advantage. Likewise, if a company is consistently showing net earnings under 10% on total revenues it is—more likely than not—in a highly competitive business in which no one company holds a durable competitive advantage. This of course leaves an enormous gray area of companies that earn between 10% and 20% on total revenue, which is just packed with businesses ripe for mining long-term investment gold that no one has yet discovered.

One of the exceptions to this rule is banks and financial companies, where an abnormally high ratio of net earnings to total revenues usually means a slacking-off in the risk management department. While the numbers look enticing, they actually indicate an acceptance of greater risk for easier money, which in the game of lending money is usually a recipe for making quick money at the cost of long-term disaster. And having financial disasters is not how one gets rich.

CHAPTER 20

PER-SHARE EARNINGS:
HOW WARREN TELLS THE
WINNERS FROM THE LOSERS

P er-share earnings are the net earnings of the company on a per-share basis for the time period in question. This is a big number in the world of investing because, as a rule, the more a company earns per share the higher its stock price is. To determine the company's per-share earnings we take the amount of net income the company earned and divide it by the number of shares it has outstanding. As an example: If a company had net earnings of $10 million for the year, and it has one million shares outstanding, it would have per-share earnings for the year of $10 a share.

While no one yearly per-share figure can be used to identify a company with a durable competitive advantage, a per-share earnings figure for a ten-year period can give us a very clear picture of whether the company has a long-term competitive advantage working in its favor. What Warren looks for is a per-share earning picture over a ten-year period that shows consistency and an upward trend.

Something that looks like this:

08	$2.95
07	$2.68
06	$2.37
05	$2.17
04	$2.06
03	$1.95
02	$1.65
01	$1.60
00	$1.48
99	$1.30
98	$1.42

This shows Warren that the company has consistent earnings with a long-term upward trend—an excellent sign that the company in question has some kind of long-term competitive advantage working in its favor. Consistent earnings are usually a sign that the company is selling a product or mix of products that don't need to go through the expensive process of change. The upward trend in earnings means that the company's economics are strong enough to allow it either to make the expenditures to increase market share through advertising or expansion, or to use financial engineering like stock buybacks.

• • •

The companies that Warren stays away from have an erratic earnings picture that looks like this:

08	$2.50
07	$(0.45) loss
06	$3.89
05	$(6.05) loss
04	$6.39
03	$5.03
02	$3.35
01	$1.77
00	$6.68
99	$8.53
98	$5.24

This shows a downward trend, punctuated by losses, which tells Warren that this company is in a fiercely competitive industry prone to booms and busts. The booms show up when demand is greater than supply, but when demand is great, the company increases production to meet demand, which increases costs and eventually leads to an excess of supply in the industry. Excess leads to falling prices, which means that the company loses money until the next boom comes along. There are thousands of companies like this, and the wild price swings in shares, caused by each company's erratic earnings, create the illusion of buying opportunities for traditional value investors. But what they are really buying is a long, slow boat ride to investor nowhere.

BALANCE SHEET

"One of the things you will find—which is interesting
and people don't think of it enough—with most
businesses and with most individuals, is life tends to
snap you at your weakest link. The two biggest weak
links in my experience: I've seen more people fail
because of liquor and leverage—leverage being
borrowed money."

—WARREN BUFFETT

CHAPTER 21

BALANCE SHEET IN GENERAL

One of the first things Warren does when he is trying to figure out if a company has a durable competitive advantage or not is to go and see how much the company has in assets— think cash and property—and how much money it owes to vendors, the banks, and the bondholders. To do this, he looks at the company's balance sheet.

Balance sheets, unlike income statements, are only for a set date. There is no such thing as a balance sheet for the year or quarter. We can create a balance sheet for any day of the year, but it will only be for that specific date. A company's accounting department will generate a balance sheet at the end of each fiscal quarter. Think of it as a snapshot of the company's financial condition on the particular date that the balance sheet is generated.

Now a balance sheet is broken into two parts: The first part is all the assets, and there are many different kinds of assets. They include cash, receivables, inventory, property, plant, and equipment.

The second part of the balance sheet is liabilities and shareholder equity.

Under liabilities we find two different categories of liabilities: Current Liabilities and Long-Term Liabilities. "Current liabilities" means the money that is owed within the year, which includes Cash and Short-Term Investments, Total Inventory, Total Receivables, and Prepaid Expenses.

Long-term liabilities are those that come due in one year or more, and include the money owed to the vendors that sold us goods, unpaid taxes, bank loans, and bond loans.

Warren, in his search for companies with a durable competitive advantage, is looking for certain things in each category of assets and liabilities, which we will get to a little later on in the book.

Now if we take all the assets and subtract all the liabilities, we will get the net worth of the business, which is the same as shareholders' equity. As an example: If the business had assets worth $100K and liabilities of $25K, then the business would have a net worth or shareholders' equity of $75K. But if the business had assets worth $100K and liabilities of $175K, the business would have negative net worth, or negative shareholders' equity, of $75K.

Assets minus Liabilities = Net Worth or Shareholders' Equity

Okay, that is the end of the balance sheet primer, so let's jump in and see how Warren uses the balance sheet and all of its subcategories to identify a company that has a durable competitive advantage over its competitors.

Balance Sheet

($ in millions)

Assets

Cash & Short-Term Investments	$4,208
Total Inventory	2,220
Total Receivables, Net	3,317
Prepaid Expenses	2,260
Other Current Assets, Total	0
Total Current Assets	12,005
Property/Plant/Equipment	8,493
Goodwill, Net	4,246
Intangibles, Net	7,863
Long-Term Investments	7,777
Other Long-Term Assets	2,675
Other Assets	0
Total Assets	$43,059

Liabilities

Accounts Payable	$1,380
Accrued Expenses	5,535
Short-Term Debt	5,919
Long-Term Debt Due	133
Other Current Liabilities	258
Total Current Liabilities	13,225
Long-Term Debt	3,277
Deferred Income Tax	1,890
Minority Interest	0
Other Liabilities	3,133
Total Liabilities	21,525

Shareholders' Equity

Preferred Stock	0
Common Stock	880
Additional Paid in Capital	7,378
Retained Earnings	36,235
Treasury Stock—Common	−23,375
Other Equity	626
Total Shareholders' Equity	21,744
Total Liabilities & Shareholders' Equity	$43,269

CHAPTER 22

ASSETS

Balance Sheet/Assets

($ in millions)

Cash & Short-Term Investments	$4,208
Total Inventory	2,220
Total Receivables, Net	3,317
Prepaid Expenses	2,260
Other Current Assets, Total	0
Total Current Assets	12,005
Property/Plant/Equipment	8,493
Goodwill, Net	4,246
Intangibles, Net	7,863
Long-Term Investments	7,777
Other Long-Term Assets	2,675
Other Assets	0
Total Assets	$43,059

This is where all the goodies are kept: the cash, the plant and equipment, the patents, and all the stuff that riches are made of. They are found on the company's balance sheet under the heading Assets.

On the balance sheet, accounting types long ago divided Corporate Assets into two distinct groups: Current Assets, and All Other Assets.

Current Assets is made up of "cash and cash equivalents," "short-term investments," "net receivables," "inventory," and a general slush fund called "other assets." These are called current assets because they are cash, or they can be or will be converted into cash in a very short period of time (usually within a year). As a rule, they are listed on the balance sheet in order of their liquidity (which means how quickly they can be turned into cash). Historically, current assets have also been called quick, liquid, or floating assets. What is important about them is their availability to be turned into cash and spent should the business economics of the enterprise start to erode and other sources of day-to-day operating capital start to evaporate. (If you can't imagine sources of operating capital evaporating overnight, just think Bear Stearns.)

All other assets are those that aren't current, which means that they will not or cannot be converted into cash in the year ahead; they are listed in a separate category immediately under

Current Assets. In this category go Long-Term Investments, Property Plant and Equipment, Goodwill, Intangible Assets, Accumulated Amortization, Other Assets, and Deferred Long-Term Asset Charges.

Collectively these two groups of assets make up the company's total assets. Individually and collectively, via their quality and quantity, they tell Warren a great many things about the economic character of a business and whether or not it possesses the coveted durable competitive advantage that will make him superrich.

This is why we are going to spend the next couple of chapters discussing the individual asset classes and how Warren uses them to identify a company with the durable competitive advantage.

So let's take a look at the categories and see how we can use them individually and collectively to help us identify the exceptional business with a long-term competitive advantage working in its favor.

CHAPTER 23

CURRENT ASSET CYCLE:
HOW THE MONEY IS MADE

Balance Sheet/Assets
($ in millions)
→ Cash & Short-Term Investments $4,208
→ Total Inventory 2,220
→ Total Receivables, Net 3,317
Prepaid Expenses 2,260
Other Current Assets, Total 0
Total Current Assets $12,005

Current assets are also referred to as the "working assets" of the business because they are in the cycle of cash going to buy inventory; Inventory is then sold to vendors and becomes Accounts Receivable. Accounts Receivable, when collected from the vendors, then turns back into Cash. Cash → Inventory → Accounts Receivable → Cash. This cycle repeats itself over and over again, and it is how a business makes money.

The different elements of the current asset cycle can tell Warren a great deal about the economic nature of the business and whether or not it has a durable competitive advantage in the marketplace.

CHAPTER 24

CASH AND CASH EQUIVALENTS: WARREN'S PILE OF LOOT

Balance Sheet/Assets

($ in millions)

→ Cash & Short-Term Investments	$4,208
→ Total Inventory	2,220
→ Total Receivables, Net	3,317
Prepaid Expenses	2,260
Other Current Assets, Total	0
Total Current Assets	$12,005

One of the first things Warren does is to look at the assets to see how much cash and cash equivalents a company has. This asset is exactly what it says it is—cash—or it is the equivalent of cash, such as a short-term CD at the bank, three-month Treasuries, or other highly liquid assets. A high number for cash or cash equivalents tells Warren one of two things—that a company has a competitive advantage that is generating tons of cash, which is a good thing, or that it has just sold a business or a ton of bonds, which may not be a good thing. A low amount or the lack of a stockpile of cash usually means that the company has poor or mediocre economics. To figure out which is which, let's look a little deeper at the asset of cash.

Companies traditionally keep a hoard of cash to support business operations. Think of it as a very large checkbook. But if we are earning more than we are spending, the cash starts to pile up and that creates the investment problem of what to do with all the excess cash. Which is a lovely problem to have.

Since cash earns a low rate of return in a bank account or CD, it is better to employ the cash assets in business operations or investments that produce a higher rate of return. What do you want to own? A short-term CD that is earning 4% on your invested money, or an apartment house that will earn you 20% on your investment? You take the apartment house. The same thing goes on in a business. The money comes in the door, and if it comes in faster than operating costs can spend it, it starts to pile up; as it piles up, the company has to decide what to do with it. Traditionally, companies have used excess cash to expand operations, buy entirely new businesses, invest in partially owned businesses via the stock market, buy back their shares, or pay out a cash dividend to shareholders. But quite often they simply sock it away for a rainy day. One can never be too financially prepared in our constantly changing and challenging world.

A company basically has three ways of creating a large stockpile of cash. It can sell new bonds or equity to the public, which creates a stockpile of cash before it is put to use. It can also sell an existing business or other assets that the company owns, which can also create a stockpile of cash before the company finds other uses for it. Or it has an ongoing business that generates more cash than the business burns. It is this scenario of a large stockpile of cash created by an ongoing business that really grabs Warren's attention. Because a company that has a surplus of cash as the result of ongoing business is often a company that has some kind of durable competitive advantage working in its favor.

When Warren is looking at a company that is suffering a short-term business problem, and causing shortsighted Wall Street to bear down on the company's shares, Warren will look at the cash or marketable securities that the company has hoarded away to give him an idea whether it has the financial strength to weather the troubles it has gotten itself into.

So here is the rule: If we see a lot of cash and marketable securities and little or no debt, chances are very good that the business will sail on through the troubled times. But if the company is hurting for cash and is sitting on a mountain of debt, it probably is a sinking ship that not even the most skilled manager can save.

A simple test to see exactly what is creating all the cash is to look at the past seven years of balance sheets. This will reveal whether the cash hoard was created by a one-time event, such as the sale of new bonds or shares, or the sale of an asset or an existing business, or whether it was created by ongoing business operations. If we see lots of debt, we probably aren't dealing with an exceptional business. But if we see a ton of cash piling up and little or no debt, and no sales of new shares or assets, and we also note a history of consistent earnings, we're probably seeing an excellent business with the durable competitive advantage that Warren is searching for—the kind of company that will make us rich over the long-term.

Lest we forget, cash is king when troubled times hit, so if we have it when our competitors don't, we get to rule.

And getting to rule is all that it is cracked up to be.

CHAPTER 25

INVENTORY: WHAT THE COMPANY NEEDS TO BUY AND WHAT THE COMPANY NEEDS TO SELL

> **Balance Sheet/Assets**
>
> ($ in millions)
>
> | | |
> |---|---|
> | Cash & Short-Term Investments | $4,208 |
> | → Total Inventory | 2,220 |
> | Total Receivables, Net | 3,317 |
> | Prepaid Expenses | 2,260 |
> | Other Current Assets, Total | 0 |
> | Total Current Assets | $12,005 |

Inventory is the company's products that it has warehoused to sell to its vendors. Since a balance sheet is always for a specific day, the amount found on the balance sheet for inventory is the value of the company's inventory for that date.

With a lot of businesses, there is a risk of inventory becoming obsolete. But as we have discussed earlier, manufacturing companies with a durable competitive advantage have an advantage, in that the products they sell never change and therefore never become obsolete. This is an advantage Warren wants to see.

When trying to identify a manufacturing company with a durable competitive advantage, look for an inventory and net earnings that are on a corresponding rise. This indicates that the company is finding profitable ways to increase sales, and that increase in sales has called for an increase in inventory, so the company can fulfill orders on time.

Manufacturing companies with inventories that rapidly ramp up for a few years and then, just as rapidly, ramp down, are more likely than not companies caught in highly competitive industries subject to booms and busts. And no one ever got rich going bust.

CHAPTER 26

NET RECEIVABLES:
MONEY OWED TO THE COMPANY

> **Balance Sheet/Assets**
>
> ($ in millions)
>
> | | |
> |---|---|
> | Cash & Short-Term Investments | $4,208 |
> | Total Inventory | 2,220 |
> | → Total Receivables, Net | 3,317 |
> | Prepaid Expenses | 2,260 |
> | Other Current Assets, Total | 0 |
> | Total Current Assets | $12,005 |

When a company sells its products to a purchaser, it does so on the basis of either cash up front or payment due thirty days after the purchaser receives the goods. In some businesses the cash isn't due for even longer periods. Sales in this state of limbo, where the cash is due, are called receivables. This is money that is owed the company. Since a certain percentage of purchasers that were sold goods will not pay, an estimated amount for bad debts is deducted from the Receivables, which gives us Net Receivables.

Receivables less Bad Debts equals Net Receivables.

Net Receivables as a stand-alone number tells us very little about the company's long-term competitive advantage. However, it does tell us a great deal about different companies within the same industry. In very competitive industries, some companies will attempt to gain an advantage by offering better payment terms—instead of 30 days, they may give vendors 120 days. This will cause an increase in sales and an increase in receivables.

If a company is consistently showing a lower percentage of Net Receivables to Gross Sales than its competitors, it usually has some kind of competitive advantage working in its favor that the others don't have.

CHAPTER 27

PREPAID EXPENSES/OTHER CURRENT ASSETS

Balance Sheet/Assets

($ in millions)

Cash & Short-Term Investments	$4,208
Total Inventory	2,220
Total Receivables, Net	3,317
→ Prepaid Expenses	2,260
→ Other Current Assets, Total	0
Total Current Assets	$12,005

Businesses sometimes pay for goods and services that they will receive in the near future, although they have not yet taken possession of the goods or received the benefits of the service. Even though the goods or services have not been received, they are paid for, so they are assets of the business. They are noted as current assets in the account for prepaid expenses. Insurance premiums for the year ahead, which are paid in advance, would be one such prepaid expense. Prepaid expenses offer us little information about the nature of the business, or about whether it is benefiting from having a durable competitive advantage.

Other current assets are non-cash assets that are due within the year but are not as yet in the company's hands. These include such things as deferred income tax recoveries, which are due within the year, but aren't cash in hand just yet.

CHAPTER 28

TOTAL CURRENT ASSETS AND THE CURRENT RATIO

Balance Sheet/Assets

($ in millions)

Cash & Short-Term Investments	$4,208
Total Inventory	2,220
Total Receivables, Net	3,317
Prepaid Expenses	2,260
Other Current Assets, Total	0
→ Total Current Assets	$12,005

Total Current Assets is a number that has long played an important role in financial analysis. Analysts have traditionally argued that subtracting a company's current liabilities from its current assets gives them an idea whether the company can meet its short-term debt obligations. They developed the current ratio, which is derived by dividing current assets by current liabilities; the higher the ratio is, the more liquid the company. A current ratio of over one is considered good, and anything below one bad. If it is below one, it is believed that the company may have a hard time meeting its short-term obligations to its creditors.

The funny thing about a lot of companies with a durable competitive advantage is that quite often their current ratio is below the magical one. Moody's comes in at .64, Coca-Cola at .95, Procter & Gamble at .82, and Anheuser-Busch at .88. Which, from an old-school perspective, means that these companies might have difficulties paying current liabilities. What is really happening is that their earning power is so strong they can easily cover their current liabilities. Also, as a result of their tremendous earning power, these companies have no problem tapping into the cheap, short-term commercial paper market if they need any additional short-term cash.

Because of their great earning power, they can also pay out generous dividends and make stock repurchases, both of which diminish cash reserves and help pull their current ratios below one. But it is the consistency of their earning power, which comes with having a durable competitive advantage, that ensures they can cover their current liabilities and not fall prey to the vicissitudes of business cycles and recessions.

In short, there are many companies with a durable competitive advantage that have current ratios less than one. Such companies create an anomaly that renders the current ratio almost useless in helping us identify whether or not a company has a durable competitive advantage.

CHAPTER 29

PROPERTY, PLANT, AND EQUIPMENT: FOR WARREN NOT HAVING THEM CAN BE A GOOD THING

Balance Sheet/Assets	
($ in millions)	
Total Current Assets	$12,005
→ Property/Plant/Equipment	8,493
Goodwill, Net	4,246
Intangibles, Net	7,863
Long-Term Investments	7,777
Other Long-Term Assets	2,675
Other Assets	0
Total Assets	$43,059

A company's property, its manufacturing plant and equipment, and their collective value are carried on the balance sheet as an asset. They are carried at their original cost, less accumulated depreciation. Depreciation is what occurs as the plant and equipment wear out little by little; every year, a charge is taken against the plant and equipment.

Companies that don't have a long-term competitive advantage are faced with constant competition, which means they constantly have to update their manufacturing facilities to try to stay competitive, often before such equipment is worn out. This, of course, creates an ongoing expense that is often quite substantial, and keeps adding to the amount of plant and equipment the company lists on its balance sheet.

A company that has a durable competitive advantage doesn't need to constantly upgrade its plant and equipment to stay competitive. Take the brand name gum manufacturer Wrigley. It builds a plant that makes chewing gum, and it doesn't have to update the plant and equipment until they wear out.

So the company that has a durable competitive advantage replaces its plant and equipment as they wear out, while the company that doesn't have a durable competitive advantage has to replace its plant and equipment to keep pace with the competition.

A company with a durable competitive advantage will be able to finance any new plants and equipment internally. But a company that doesn't have a competitive advantage will be forced to turn to debt to finance its constant need to retool its plants to keep up with the competition.

We see this when we take a company with a long-term competitive advantage like Wrigley, which has plant and equipment worth $1.4 billion, carries $1 billion in debt, and earns in the neighborhood of $500 million per year. Compare Wrigley with a company without a durable competitive advantage, like GM, which has plant and equipment valued at $56 billion, carries $40 billion in debt, and has lost money for the last two years.

Chewing gum is not a product that changes much, and Wrigley's brand name ensures a competitive advantage over its rivals. But GM must compete head-on with every car manufacturer on the planet, and its product mix constantly has to be upgraded and redesigned to stay ahead of the competition. This means that GM's plants have to regularly be retooled to produce the new products.

Making chewing gum is a much better and a far more profitable business for shareholders than making cars. Consider this: $100,000 invested in Wrigley back in 1990 would be worth approximately $547,000 in 2008. But $100,000 invested in GM back in 1990 would be worth approximately $97,000 in 2008. This equates to a difference of $460,000 in Wrigley's shareholders' favor. They have happily chewed their way to riches, while GM's shareholders have watched their fortunes drive off a cliff.

As Warren says, producing a consistent product that doesn't have to change equates to consistent profits. The consistent product means there is no need to spend tons of money upgrading the plant and equipment just to stay competitive, which frees up tons of money for other money-making ventures. To get rich, we first have to make money, and it helps if we make lots of money. One of the ways to make lots of money is not having to spend a ton of money keeping up with the Joneses.

CHAPTER 30

GOODWILL

Balance Sheet/Assets	
($ in millions)	
Total Current Assets	$12,005
Property/Plant/Equipment	8,493
→ Goodwill, Net	4,246
Intangibles, Net	7,863
Long-Term Investments	7,777
Other Long-Term Assets	2,675
Total Assets	$43,059

When Exxon buys XYZ oil company and Exxon pays a price in excess of XYZ's book value, the excess is recorded on Exxon's balance sheet under the heading of Goodwill. Buy a lot of companies for a price in excess of their book value, and we end up with a lot of goodwill on our balance sheet.

Goodwill used to be written off against the earnings of the business through a process of amortization, which caused a yearly charge against earnings on the income statement under the title of amortization of goodwill. In the modern age, the FASB (Financial Accounting Standards Board) decided that goodwill wouldn't have to be amortized unless the company that the goodwill was attached to was actually depreciating in value.

Whenever we see an increase in goodwill of a company over a number of years, we can assume that it is because the company is out buying other businesses. This can be a good thing if the company is buying businesses that also have a durable competitive advantage. If the goodwill account stays the same year after year, that is because either the company is paying under book value for a business or the company isn't making any acquisitions.

Businesses that benefit from some kind of durable competitive advantage almost never sell for below their book value. We say almost never, but occasionally it does happen, and when it does, it can be the buying opportunity of a lifetime.

CHAPTER 31

INTANGIBLE ASSETS:
MEASURING THE UNMEASURABLE

Balance Sheet/Assets	
($ in millions)	
Total Current Assets	$12,005
Property/Plant/Equipment	8,493
Goodwill, Net	4,246
→ Intangibles, Net	7,863
Long-Term Investments	7,777
Other Long-Term Assets	2,675
Total Assets	$43,059

Intangible assets are assets we can't physically touch; these include patents, copyrights, trademarks, franchises, brand names, and the like. A long time ago, a company could slap on to its intangibles any old valuation it thought it could get away with. Which made for some very interesting valuations and many abuses. In the current era, companies are not allowed to carry internally developed intangible assets on their balance sheets. That's put an end to watering the balance sheet with fantasy valuations for intangible assets.

However, intangible assets that are acquired from a third party are carried on the balance sheet at their fair value. If an asset has a finite life—as a patent does—it is amortized over the course of its useful life with a yearly charge made to the income statement and the balance sheet.

An odd thing occurs with companies that benefit from a durable competitive advantage. Take the Coca-Cola Company for an example. Coke's brand name is worth in excess of $100 billion, yet because it is an internally developed brand name, its real value as an intangible asset is not reflected on Coca-Cola's balance sheet. The same thing applies to Wrigley, Pepsi Co., McDonald's, and even Wal-Mart. Each of these companies benefits from having durable competitive advantage tied directly to its name; yet the value of their greatest asset, their name, isn't recognized on their balance sheets.

This is one of the reasons that the durable competitive advantage's power to increase shareholders' wealth has remained hidden from investors for so long. Short of comparing ten years' worth of income statements, investors have had no way of knowing it was there, or knowing of its potential for making them superrich. This is how Warren was able to take large positions in such visible companies, like Coca-Cola, with the whole world watching. Yet the whole world had no clue why he was doing it. Coke was too pricey to make any sense to the value investors that followed Graham, and its price wasn't volatile enough to be interesting to Wall Street traders. What Warren could see, that no one else could, was Coke's durable competitive advantage and the long-term earning power that came with it. Earning power that, over time, would help make him the richest man in the world.

CHAPTER 32

LONG-TERM INVESTMENTS: ONE OF THE SECRETS TO WARREN'S SUCCESS

Balance Sheet/Assets	
($ in millions)	
Total Current Assets	$12,005
Property/Plant/Equipment	8,493
Goodwill, Net	4,246
Intangibles, Net	7,863
→ Long-Term Investments	7,777
Other Long-Term Assets	2,675
Total Assets	$43,059

This is an asset account on a company's balance sheet, where the value of long-term investments (longer than a year), such as stocks, bonds, and real estate is recorded. This account includes investments in the company's affiliates and subsidiaries. What is interesting about the long-term investment account is that this asset class is carried on the books at their cost or market price, whichever is lower. But it cannot be marked to a price above cost even if the investments have appreciated in value. This means that a company can have a very valuable asset that it is carrying on its books at a valuation considerably below its market price.

A company's long-term investments can tell us a lot about the investment mind-set of top management. Do they invest in other businesses that have durable competitive advantages, or do they invest in businesses that are in highly competitive markets? Sometimes we see the management of a wonderful business making huge investments in mediocre businesses for no other reason than they think big is better. Sometimes we see some enlightened manager of a mediocre business making investments in companies that have a durable competitive advantage. This is how Warren built his holding company Berkshire Hathaway into the empire that it is today. Berkshire was once-upon-a-time a mediocre business in the highly competitive textile industry. Warren bought a controlling interest, stopped paying the dividend so cash would accumulate, and then took the company's working capital and went and bought an insurance company. Then he took the assets of the insurance company and went on a forty-year shopping spree for companies with a durable competitive advantage.

Kiss even a frog of a business enough times with a durable competitive advantage and it will turn into a prince of a business.

Or, as in Warren's case, $60 billion, which is what his stock in Berkshire is now worth.

CHAPTER 33

OTHER LONG-TERM ASSETS

Balance Sheet/Assets	
($ in millions)	
Total Current Assets	$12,005
Property/Plant/Equipment	8,493
Goodwill, Net	4,246
Intangibles, Net	7,863
Long-Term Investments	7,777
→ Other Long-Term Assets	2,675
Total Assets	$43,059

Think of "other long-term assets" as a giant pool of long-term assets—assets that have useful lives of greater than a year—that didn't make it into the categories of Property and Equipment, Goodwill, Intangibles, and Long-Term Investments. An example of Other Long-Term Assets would be prepaid expenses and tax recoveries that are due to be received in the coming years.

There is little that Other Long-Term Assets can tell us about whether or not the company in question has a durable competitive advantage. So let's move on.

CHAPTER 34

TOTAL ASSETS AND
THE RETURN ON TOTAL ASSETS

Balance Sheet/Assets	
($ in millions)	
Total Current Assets	$12,005
Property/Plant/Equipment	8,493
Goodwill, Net	4,246
Intangibles, Net	7,863
Long-Term Investments	7,777
Other Long-Term Assets	2,675
→ Total Assets	$43,059

Add current assets to long-term assets, and we get the company's total assets. Its total assets will match its total liabilities, plus shareholders' equity. They balance with each other, which is why it is called a balance sheet.

Total assets are important in determining just how efficient the company is in putting its assets to use. To measure the company's efficiency, analysts have come up with the return on asset ratio, which is found by dividing net earnings by total assets.

Capital, however, always presents a barrier to entry into any industry, and one of the things that helps make a company's competitive advantage durable is the cost of the assets one needs to get into the game. Coca-Cola has $43 billion in assets and a return on assets of 12%; Procter & Gamble has $143 billion in assets and a return on assets of 7%; and Altria Group, Inc., has $52 billion in assets and a return on assets of 24%. But a company like Moody's, which has $1.7 billion in assets, shows a 43% return on assets.

While many analysts argue that the higher the return on assets the better, Warren has discovered that really high returns on assets may indicate vulnerability in the durability of the company's competitive advantage. Raising $43 billion to take on Coca-Cola is an impossible task—it's not going to happen. But raising $1.7 billion to take on Moody's is within the realm of possibility. While Moody's underlying economics is far superior to Coca-Cola's, the durability of Moody's competitive advantage is far weaker because of the lower cost of entry into its business.

The lesson here is that sometimes more can actually mean less over the long-term.

CHAPTER 35

CURRENT LIABILITIES

Balance Sheet/Liabilities	
($ in millions)	
Accounts Payable	$1,380
Accrued Expenses	5,535
Short-Term Debt	5,919
Long-Term Debt Due	133
Other Current Liabilities	258
Total Current Liabilities	$13,225

Current liabilities are the debts and obligations that the company owes that are coming due within the fiscal year. They are found on the balance sheet under the headings of Accounts Payable, Accrued Expenses, Short-Term Debt, Long-Term Debt Coming Due, and Other Current Liabilities. Let's take a look at them and see what they can tell us about whether or not a company has a durable competitive advantage over its competitors.

CHAPTER 36

ACCOUNTS PAYABLE, ACCRUED EXPENSES, AND OTHER CURRENT LIABILITIES

Balance Sheet/Liabilities	
($ in millions)	
→ Accounts Payable	$1,380
→ Accrued Expenses	5,535
Short-Term Debt	5,919
Long-Term Debt Due	133
→ Other Current Liabilities	258
Total Current Liabilities	$13,225

Accounts payable is money owed to suppliers that have provided goods and services to the company on credit. We order 1,000 pounds of coffee, and they send it to us along with a bill/invoice. The bill/invoice for the 1,000 pounds of coffee is an account payable.

Accrued expenses are liabilities that the company has

incurred, but has yet to be invoiced for. These expenses include sales tax payable, wages payable, and accrued rent payable. We hire someone and tell him that we will pay him at the end of the month; each day that he works 'til the end of the month is booked as an accrued expense.

Other debts is a slush fund for all short-term debts that didn't qualify to be included in any of the above categories.

Accounts Payable, Accrued Expenses, and Other Debts can tell us a lot about the current situation of a business, but as stand-alone entries they tell us little about the long-term economic nature of the business and whether or not it has a durable competitive advantage. However, the amount of short- and long-term debt that a company carries can tell a great deal about the long-term economics of a business and whether or not it has a durable competitive advantage.

CHAPTER 37

SHORT-TERM DEBT: HOW IT CAN KILL A FINANCIAL INSTITUTION

Balance Sheet/Liabilities	
($ in millions)	
Accounts Payable	$1,380
Accrued Expenses	5,535
→ Short-Term Debt	5,919
Long-Term Debt Due	133
Other Current Liabilities	258
Total Current Liabilities	$13,225

Short-term debt is money that is owed by the corporation and due within the year. This includes commercial paper and short-term bank loans. Short-term money historically has been cheaper than long-term money. This means that it is possible to make money borrowing short-term and lending it long-term. We borrow short-term money at 5% and lend it long-term for 7%—sounds easy enough. But the problem with this strategy is that the money we borrowed is short-term money. That means that we have to pay it back within the year, which is easy enough to do—we just borrow more money short-term to pay back the short-term debt that is coming due. In the financial world, this is called "rolling over the debt." And it all works well until short-term rates jump above what we lent the money long at, which was 7%. Sure, it seemed like a great idea when short-term rates were 5%, but now that they have jumped to 8%, we have to refinance our short-term debt at a rate in excess of what we loaned it out at. And that does not make us happy.

Another part of the short-term borrowing disaster equation is what happens if we lend all this money long-term, but our creditors decide not to loan us any more money short-term. Suddenly we have to pay back all that money we borrowed short-term and lent long-term. But we don't have it, because we lent it long-term, which means that we won't get paid back for many, many years.

This is what happened to Bear Stearns: They borrowed short-term and bought mortgage-backed securities, using the mortgage-backed securities as collateral for the short-term loans. But one day their creditors woke up and said, "We don't think the collateral is worth what you guys told us it was worth, so we don't want to lend you any more money and we want to collect the money we did loan you." Not a good position for Bear Stearns to be in.

The smartest and safest way to make money in banking is to borrow it long-term and lend it long-term. That's why banks are always trying to lock us into those five- and ten-year CDs. It is not the fast and easy money of borrowing short-term and lending it long, but it is a saner and far more conservative way to make money. Which is what we want in a bank and a banker—sanity.

When it comes to investing in financial institutions Warren has always shied away from companies that are bigger borrowers of short-term money than of long-term money. Warren's favorite, Wells Fargo, has 57 cents of short-term debt for every dollar of long-term debt. But an aggressive bank, like Bank of America N.A., has $2.09 of short-term debt for every dollar of long-term debt. And while being aggressive can mean making lots of money over the short-term, it has often led to financial disasters over the long-term. And one never gets rich being on the downside of a financial disaster.

In troubled financial times it is the stable conservative banks like Wells Fargo that have the competitive advantage over the go-go aggressive banks that have gotten themselves into trouble. The "durability" equates with the stability that comes with being conservative. It has money when the others have losses, which creates opportunity. Aggressive borrowers of short-term money are often at the mercy of sudden shifts in the credit markets, which puts their entire operation at risk and equates with a loss of any kind of durability in their business model. And in the business world durability of a competitive advantage is a lot like virginity—easier to protect than it is to get back.

CHAPTER 38

LONG-TERM DEBT COMING DUE
AND THE TROUBLES IT CAN CAUSE

Balance Sheet/Liabilities	
($ in millions)	
Accounts Payable	$1,380
Accrued Expenses	5,535
Short-Term Debt	5,919
→ Long-Term Debt Due	133
Other Current Liabilities	258
Total Current Liabilities	$13,225

This chapter concerns long-term debt that is coming due and has to be paid off in the current year. Long-term debt is not a yearly current liability for most businesses. However, a few very large corporations do have some portion of their long-term debt coming due on a yearly basis. Where it can create problems is when some companies lump it in with short-term debt on the balance sheet, which creates the illusion that the company has more short-term debt than it really does.

As a rule, companies with a durable competitive advantage require little or no long-term debt to maintain their business operations, and therefore have little or no long-term debt ever coming due. So if we are dealing with a company that has a lot of long-term debt coming due, we probably aren't dealing with a company that has a long-term competitive advantage.

Any time we are buying into a company that has a durable competitive advantage but has been going through troubled times due to a one-time solvable event—like a subsidiary in a different business bleeding cash—it is best to check the horizon and see how much of the company's long-term debt is due in the years ahead. Too much debt coming due in a single year can spook investors, which will give us a lower price to buy in at.

With a mediocre company that is experiencing serious problems, too much debt coming due in a current year can lead to cash flow problems and certain bankruptcy, which is also certain death to our investment.

And having dying investments is not how we get rich.

CHAPTER 39

TOTAL CURRENT LIABILITIES
AND THE CURRENT RATIO

Balance Sheet/Liabilities

($ in millions)

Accounts Payable	$1,380
Accrued Expenses	5,535
Short-Term Debt	5,919
Long-Term Debt Due	133
Other Current Liabilities	258
→ Total Current Liabilities	$13,225

By dividing Total Current Assets by Total Current Liabilities, one can determine the liquidity of the company—the higher the current ratio, the more liquid the company is, and the greater its ability to pay current liabilities when they come due. A current ratio of over one is considered good, and anything below one, bad. If it is below one, it is thought that the company might have a hard time meeting its short-term obligations to its creditors. But, as we discussed in Chapter 28, companies with a durable competitive advantage often have current ratios under one. What causes this anomaly is the immense earning power the durable competitive advantage creates. In short, you have a current economic picture that doesn't require the "liquidity cushion" that a company with poorer economics needs. (For a more in-depth discussion, please refer back to Chapter 28.) While the current ratio is of great importance in determining the liquidity of a marginal-to-average business, it is of little use in telling us whether or not a company has a durable competitive advantage.

CHAPTER 40

LONG-TERM DEBT:
SOMETHING THAT GREAT COMPANIES
DON'T HAVE A LOT OF

Balance Sheet/Liabilities

($ in millions)

Total Current Liabilities	$13,225
→ Long-Term Debt	3,277
Deferred Income Tax	1,890
Minority Interest	0
Other Liabilities	3,133
Total Liabilities	$21,525

Long-term debt means debt that matures any time out past a year. On the balance sheet it comes under the heading of long-term liabilities. If the debt comes due within the year, it is short-term debt and is placed with the company's current liabilities. In Warren's search for the excellent business with a long-term competitive advantage, the amount of long-term debt a company carries on its books tells him a lot about the economic nature of the business.

Warren has learned that companies that have a durable competitive advantage often carry little or no long-term debt on their balance sheets. This is because these companies are so profitable that they are self-financing when they need to expand the business or make acquisitions, so there is never a need to borrow large sums of money.

One of the ways to help us identify the exceptional business, then, is to check how much long-term debt it is carrying on its balance sheet. We are not just interested in the current year; we want to look at the long-term debt load that the company has been carrying for the last ten years. If there have been ten years of operations with little or no long-term debt on the company's balance sheet it is a good bet that the company has some kind of strong competitive advantage working in its favor.

Warren's historic purchases indicate that on any given year the company should have sufficient yearly net earnings to pay off all of its long-term debt within a three- or four-year earnings period. Long-term competitive advantage holders Coca-Cola and Moody's could pay off all their long-term debt in a single year; and Wrigley and The Washington Post companies can do it in two.

But companies like GM or Ford, both in the highly competitive auto industry, could spend every dime of net profit they have earned in the last ten years and still not pay off the massive amount of long-term debt they carry on their balance sheets.

The bottom line here is that companies that have enough earning power to pay off their long-term debt in under three or four years are good candidates in our search for the excellent business with a long-term competitive advantage.

But please note: Because these companies are so profitable and carrying little or no debt, they are often the targets of leveraged buyouts. This is where the buyer borrows huge amounts of money against the cash flow of the company to finance the purchase. After the leveraged buyout the business is then saddled with large amounts of debt. This was the case with the RJR/Nabisco buyout in the late 1980s.

If all else indicates that the business in question is a company with a durable competitive advantage, but it has a ton of debt on its balance sheet, a leveraged buyout may have created the debt. In cases like these the company's bonds are often the better bet, in that the company's earning power will be focused on paying off the debt and not growing the company.

The rule here is simple: Little or No Long-Term Debt Often Means a Good Long-Term Bet.

CHAPTER 41

DEFERRED INCOME TAX, MINORITY INTEREST, AND OTHER LIABILITIES

Balance Sheet/Liabilities

($ in millions)

Total Current Liabilities	$13, 225
Long-Term Debt	3,277
→ Deferred Income Tax	1,890
→ Minority Interest	0
→ Other Liabilities	3,133
Total Liabilities	$21,525

Deferred Income Tax is tax that is due but hasn't been paid. This figure tells us little about whether or not the company has a durable competitive advantage.

The Minority Interest entry on a balance sheet is far more interesting. When the company acquires the stock of another, it books the price it paid for the stock as an asset under "long-term investments." But when it acquires more than 80% of the stock of a company, it can shift the acquired company's entire balance sheet onto its balance sheet. The same with the income statement. An example: Berkshire's acquisition of 90% of the Nebraska Furniture Mart. Because it acquired more than 80% of the NFM, Berkshire could book 100% of NFM's income onto Berkshire's income statement, and it could add 100% of NFM's assets and liabilities to its balance sheet. What the Minority Interest entry represents is the value of the 10% of NFM that Berkshire does not own. This shows up as a liability to balance the equation, since Berkshire booked 100% of NFM's assets and liabilities, even though it owns only 90% of NFM. So what does this have to do with identifying a company with a durable competitive advantage? Not much, but it is interesting to know what matters and what doesn't in our search for the company with a durable competitive advantage.

"Other Liabilities" is a catchall category into which businesses pool their miscellaneous debt. It includes such liabilities as judgments against the company, non-current benefits, interest on tax liabilities, unpaid fines, and derivative instruments. None of these helps us in our search for the durable competitive advantage.

CHAPTER 42

TOTAL LIABILITIES AND THE DEBT TO SHAREHOLDERS' EQUITY RATIO

Balance Sheet/
Debt to Shareholders' Equity Ratio

($ in millions)

Total Current Liabilities	$13, 225
Long-Term Debt	3,277
Deferred Income Tax	1,890
Minority Interest	0
Other Liabilities	3,133
→ Total Liabilities	$21,525

Total liabilities is the sum of all the liabilities of the company. It is an important number that can be used to give us the debt to shareholders' equity ratio, which, with slight modification, can be used to help us identify whether or not a business has a durable competitive advantage.

The debt to shareholders' equity ratio has historically been used to help us identify whether or not a company is using debt to finance its operations or equity (which includes retained earnings). The company with a durable competitive advantage will be using its earning power to finance its operations and therefore, in theory, should show a higher level of shareholders' equity and a lower level of total liabilities. The company without a competitive advantage will be using debt to finance its operations and, therefore, should show just the opposite, a lower level of shareholders' equity and a higher level of total liabilities.

The equation is: Debt to Shareholders' Equity Ratio = Total Liabilities ÷ Shareholders' Equity.

The problem with using the debt to equity ratio as an identifier is that the economics of companies with a durable competitive advantage are so great that they don't need a large amount of equity/retained earnings on their balance sheets to get the job done; in some cases they don't need any. Because of their great earning power they will often spend their built-up equity/retained earnings on buying back their stock, which decreases their equity/retained earnings base. That in turn increases their debt to equity ratio, often to the point that their debt to equity ratio looks like that of a mediocre business—one without a durable competitive advantage.

Moody's, a Warren favorite, is an excellent example of this phenomenon. It has such great economics working in its favor that it doesn't need to maintain any shareholders' equity. It actually spent all of its shareholders' equity on buying back its shares. It literally has negative shareholders' equity. This means that its debt to shareholders' equity ratio looks more like that of GM—a company without a durable competitive advantage and a negative net worth—than, say, that of Coca-Cola, a company with a durable competitive advantage.

However, if we add back into Moody's shareholders' equity the value of all the treasury stock that Moody has acquired through stock buybacks, then Moody's debt to equity ratio drops down to .63, in line with Coke's treasury share-adjusted ratio of .51. GM still has a negative net worth, even with the addition of the value of its treasury shares, which are nonexistent because GM doesn't have the money to buy back its shares.

It is easy to see the contrast between companies with a durable competitive advantage and those without it when we look at the treasury share-adjusted debt to shareholders' equity ratio. Durable competitive advantage holder Procter & Gamble has an adjusted ratio of .71; Wrigley, meanwhile, has a ratio of .68—which means that for every dollar of shareholders' equity Wrigley has, it also has 68 cents in debt. Contrast P&G and Wrigley with Goodyear Tire, which has an adjusted ratio of 4.35, or Ford, which has an adjusted ratio of 38.0. This means that for every dollar of shareholders' equity that Ford has, it also has $38 in debt—which equates to $7.2 billion in shareholders' equity and $275 billion in debt.

With financial institutions like banks, the ratios, on average, tend to be much higher than those of their manufacturing cousins. Banks borrow tremendous amounts of money and then loan it all back out, making money on the spread between what they paid for the money and what they can loan it out for. This leads to an enormous amount of liabilities, which are offset by a tremendous amount of assets. On average, the big American money center banks have $10 in liabilities for every dollar of shareholders' equity they keep on their books. This is what Warren means when he says that banks are highly leveraged operations. There are exceptions though and one of them is M&T Bank, a longtime Warren favorite. M&T has a ratio of 7.7, which is reflective of its management's more conservative lending practices.

The simple rule here is that, unless we are looking at a financial institution, any time we see an adjusted debt to shareholders' equity ratio below .80 (the lower the better), there is a good chance that the company in question has the coveted durable competitive advantage we are looking for.

And finding what one is looking for is always a good thing, especially if one is looking to get rich.

CHAPTER 43

SHAREHOLDERS' EQUITY/BOOK VALUE

Balance Sheet/Shareholders' Equity	
($ in millions)	
Total Liabilities	$21,525
Preferred Stock	0
Common Stock	880
Additional Paid in Capital	7,378
Retained Earnings	36,235
Treasury Stock—Common	−23,375
Other Equity	626
→ Total Shareholders' Equity	21,744
Total Liabilities & Shareholders' Equity	$43,269

When you subtract all your liabilities from all your assets you get your net worth. If you take a company's total assets and subtract its total liabilities you get the net worth of the company, which is also known as the shareholders' equity or book value of the business. This is the amount of money that the company's owners/shareholders have initially put in and have left in the business to keep it running. Shareholders' Equity is accounted for under the headings of Capital Stock, which includes Preferred and Common Stock; Paid in Capital, and Retained Earnings. Add together Total Liabilities and Total Shareholders' Equity and you get a sum that should equal Total Assets, which is why it is called a balance sheet— both sides balance.

Why Shareholders' Equity is an important number to us is that it allows us to calculate the return on shareholders' equity, which is one of the ways we determine whether or not the company in question has a long-term competitive advantage working in its favor.

Let's check it out.

CHAPTER 44

PREFERRED AND COMMON STOCK: ADDITIONAL PAID IN CAPITAL

Shareholders' Equity	
($ in millions)	
→ Preferred Stock	$0
→ Common Stock	880
→ Additional Paid in Capital	7,378
Retained Earnings	36,235
Treasury Stock—Common	−23,375
Other Equity	626
Total Shareholders' Equity	$21,744

A company can raise new capital by selling bonds or stock (equity) to the public. The money raised by selling bonds has to be paid back at some point in the future. It is borrowed money. But when the company raises money selling preferred or common stock (which is called "equity") to the public, it never has to be paid back. This money is the company's forever, to do with as it pleases.

Common stock represents ownership in the company. Common stock owners are the owners of the company and have the right to elect a board of directors, which, in turn, will hire a CEO to run the company. Common stockholders receive dividends if the board of directors votes to pay them. And if the entire company is sold, it is the common stockholders who get all the loot.

There is a second class of equity, called preferred stock. Preferred shareholders don't have voting rights, but they do have a right to a fixed or adjustable dividend that must be paid before the common stock owners receive a dividend. Preferred shareholders also have priority over common shareholders in the event that the company falls into bankruptcy.

From a balance sheet perspective preferred and common stocks are carried on the books at their par value, and any money in excess of par that was paid in when the company sold the stock will be carried on the books as "paid in capital." So if the company's preferred stock has a par value of $100/share, and it sold it to the public at $120 a share, a $100-a-share will be carried on the books under preferred stock, and $20 a share will be carried under paid in capital.

The same thing applies to common stock, with, say, a par

value of $1 a share. If it is sold to the public at $10 a share, it will be booked on the balance sheet as $1 a share under common stock and $9 a share under paid in capital.

The odd thing about preferred stock is that companies that have a durable competitive advantage tend not to have any. This is in part because they tend not to have any debt. They make so much money that they are self-financing. And while preferred stock is technically equity, in that the original money received by the company never has to be paid back, it functions like debt in that dividends have to be paid out. But unlike the interest paid on debt, which is deductible from pretax income, the dividends paid on preferred stock are not deductible, which tends to make issuing preferred shares very expensive money. Because it is expensive money, companies like to stay away from it if they can. So one of the markers we look for in our search for a company with a durable competitive advantage is the absence of preferred stock in its capital structure.

CHAPTER 45

RETAINED EARNINGS: WARREN'S SECRET FOR GETTING SUPERRICH

Balance Sheet/Shareholders' Equity	
($ in millions)	
Preferred Stock	$0
Common Stock	880
Additional Paid in Capital	7,378
→ Retained Earnings	36,235
Treasury Stock—Common	−23,375
Other Equity	626
Total Shareholders' Equity	$21,744

At the end of the day, a company's net earnings can either be paid out as dividends or used to buy back the company's shares, or they can be retained to keep the business growing. When they are retained in the business, they are added to an account on the balance sheet, under shareholders' equity, called retained earnings.

If the earnings are retained and profitably put to use, they can greatly improve the long-term economic picture of the business. It was Warren's policy of retaining 100% of Berkshire's net earnings that helped drive its shareholders' equity from $19 a share in 1965 to $78,000 a share in 2007.

To find the yearly net earnings that are going to be added to the company's retained earnings pool, we take the company's after-tax net earnings and deduct the amount that the company paid out in dividends and the expenditures in buying back stock that it had during the year. In 2007 Coca-Cola had after-tax net earnings of $5.9 billion and paid out in dividends and stock buybacks $3.1 billion. This gave the company approximately $2.8 billion in earnings, which were added to the retained earnings pool.

Retained Earnings is an accumulated number, which means that each year's new retained earnings are added to the total of accumulated retained earnings from all prior years. Likewise, if the company loses money, the loss is subtracted from what the company has accumulated in the past. If the company loses more money than it has accumulated, the retained earnings number will show up as negative.

Out of all the numbers on a balance sheet that can help us determine whether the company has a durable competitive advantage, this is one of the most important. It is important in that if a company is not making additions to its retained earnings, it is not growing its net worth. If it not growing its net worth, it is unlikely to make any of us superrich over the long run.

Simply put, the rate of growth of a company's retained earnings is a good indicator whether or not it is benefiting from having a durable competitive advantage. Let's check out a few of Warren's favorite companies with a durable competitive advantage: Coca-Cola has been growing its retained earnings pool for the last five years at an annual rate of 7.9%, Wrigley at a very chewy 10.9%, Burlington Northern Santa Fe Railway at a smoking 15.6%, Anheuser-Busch at a foamy 6.4%, Wells Fargo at a very bankable 14.2%, and Warren's very own Berkshire Hathaway at an outstanding 23%.

Not all growth in retained earnings is due to an incremental increase in sales of existing products; some of it is due to the acquisitions of other businesses. When two companies merge, their retained earnings pools are joined, which creates an even larger pool. As an example, Procter & Gamble, in 2005, saw its retained earnings jump from $13 billion to $31 billion when it merged with The Gillette Co.

Even more interesting is the fact that both General Motors and Microsoft show negative retained earnings. General Motors shows a negative number because of the poor economics of the auto business, which causes the company to lose billions. Microsoft shows a negative number because it decided that its economic engine is so powerful that it doesn't need to retain the massive amount of capital it has collected over the years and has instead chosen to spend its accumulated retained earnings and more on stock buybacks and dividend payments to its shareholders.

One of the great secrets of Warren's success with Berkshire Hathaway is that he stopped its dividend payments the day that he took control of the company. This allowed 100% of the company's yearly net earnings to be added into the retained earnings pool. As opportunities showed up, he invested the company's retained earnings in businesses that earned even more money, and that money was all added back into the retained earnings pool and eventually invested in even more money-making operations. As time went on, Berkshire's growing pool of retained earnings increased its ability to make more and more money. From 1965 to 2007, Berkshire's expanding pool of retained earnings helped grow its pretax earnings from $4 a share in 1965 to $13,023 a share in 2007, which equates to an average annual growth rate of approximately 21%.

The theory is simple: the more earnings that a company retains, the faster it grows its retained earnings pool, which, in turn will increase the growth rate for future earnings. The catch is, of course, that it has to keep buying companies that have a durable competitive advantage. Which is exactly what Warren has done with Berkshire Hathaway. Berkshire is like a goose that not only keeps laying golden eggs, but each one of those golden eggs hatches another goose with the golden touch, and those golden geese lay even more golden eggs. Warren has discovered that if you keep this process going on long enough, eventually you get to start counting your net worth in terms of billions, instead of just millions.

CHAPTER 46

TREASURY STOCK:*
WARREN LIKES TO SEE THIS ON THE
BALANCE SHEET

Balance Sheet/Shareholders' Equity	
($ in millions)	
Preferred Stock	$0
Common Stock	880
Additional Paid in Capital	7,378
Retained Earnings	36,235
→ Treasury Stock—Common	−23,375
Other Equity	626
Total Shareholders' Equity	$21,744

---

*What is known as treasury stock in the United States is referred to as treasury shares in the United Kingdom.

When a company buys back its own shares, it can do two things with them. It can cancel them or it can retain them with the possibility of reissuing them later on. If it cancels them the shares cease to exist. But if it keeps them, with the possibility of reissuing them later on, they are carried on the balance sheet under shareholders' equity as treasury stock. Shares held as treasury stock have no voting rights, nor do they receive dividends and, though arguably an asset, they are carried on the balance sheet at a negative value because they represent a reduction in the shareholders' equity.

Companies with a durable competitive advantage, because of their great economics, tend to have lots of free cash that they can spend on buying back their shares. Thus one of the hallmarks of a company with a durable competitive advantage is the presence of treasury shares on the balance sheet.

There are a several other financial dynamics to be aware of regarding treasury shares. One is that when a company buys its own shares, and holds them as treasury stock, it is effectively decreasing the company's equity, which increases the company's return on shareholders' equity. Since a high return on shareholders' equity is one sign of a durable competitive advantage, it is good to know if the high returns on equity are being generated by financial engineering or exceptional business economics or because of a combination of the two.

To see which is which, convert the negative value of the treasury shares into a positive number and add it to the shareholders' equity instead of subtracting it. Then divide the company's net earnings by the new total shareholders' equity. This will give us the company's return on equity minus the effects of financial engineering.

Also, in the United States, in determining whether or not the personal holding company tax applies, treasury shares are not part of the pool of the outstanding shares, when it comes to determining control of the company. Unscrupulous types will represent to the IRS that they only own 49% of all outstanding shares. But if they subtract the treasury shares, as the law says they should, they really control in excess of 50%, which gives them control of the business and potentially makes them liable to the personal holding company tax.

Let us leave this chapter with a simple rule: The presence of treasury shares on the balance sheet, and a history of buying back shares, are good indicators that the company in question has a durable competitive advantage working in its favor.

CHAPTER 47

RETURN ON SHAREHOLDERS' EQUITY: PART ONE

Balance Sheet/Shareholders' Equity	
($ in millions)	
Preferred Stock	$0
Common Stock	880
Additional Paid in Capital	7,378
Retained Earnings	36,235
Treasury Stock—Common	−23,375
Other Equity	626
Total Shareholders' Equity	$21,744

Shareholders' equity is equal to the company's total assets minus its total liabilities. That happens to equal the total sums of preferred and common stock, plus paid in capital, plus retained earnings, less treasury stock.

Shareholders' equity has three sources. One is the capital that was originally raised selling preferred and common stock to the public. The second is any later sales of preferred and common stock to the public after the company is up and running. The third, and most important to us, is the accumulation of retained earnings.

Since all equity belongs to the company, and since the company belongs to the common shareholders, the equity really belongs to the common shareholders, which is why it is called shareholders' equity.

Now if we are shareholders in a company, we would be very interested in how good a job management does at allocating our money, so we can earn even more. If they are bad at it we won't be very happy and might even sell our shares and put our money elsewhere. But if they are really good at it we might even buy more of the company, along with everyone else who is impressed with management's ability to profitably put shareholders' equity to good use. To this end, financial analysts developed the return on shareholders' equity equation to test management's efficiency in allocating the shareholders' money. This is an equation that Warren puts great stock in, in his search for the company with a durable competitive advantage, and it is the topic of our next chapter.

CHAPTER 48

RETURN ON SHAREHOLDERS' EQUITY: PART TWO

Calculation: Net Earnings divided by Shareholders' Equity equals Return on Shareholders' Equity.

What Warren discovered is that companies that benefit from a durable or long-term competitive advantage show higher-than-average returns on shareholders' equity. Warren's favorite, Coca-Cola, shows a return on shareholders' equity of 30%; Wrigley comes in at 24%; Hershey's earns a delicious 33%; and Pepsi measures in at 34%.

Shift over to a highly competitive business like the airlines, where no one company has a sustainable competitive advantage, and return on equity sinks dramatically. United Airlines, in a year that it makes money, comes in at 15%, and American Airlines earns 4%. Delta Air Lines and Northwest don't earn anything because they don't earn any money.

High returns on equity mean that the company is making good use of the earnings that it is retaining. As time goes by, these high returns on equity will add up and increase the underlying value of the business, which, over time, will eventually be recognized by the stock market through an increasing price for the company's stock.

Please note: Some companies are so profitable that they don't need to retain any earnings, so they pay them all out to the shareholders. In these cases we will sometimes see a negative number for shareholders' equity. The danger here is that insolvent companies will also show a negative number for shareholders' equity. If the company shows a long history of strong net earnings, but shows a negative shareholders' equity, it is probably a company with a durable competitive advantage. If the company shows both negative shareholders' equity and a history of negative net earnings, we are probably dealing with a mediocre business that is getting beaten up by the competition.

So here is the rule: High returns on shareholders' equity means "come play." Low returns on shareholders' equity mean "stay away."

Got it? Okay, let's move on.

CHAPTER 49

The Problem with Leverage and the Tricks It Can Play on You

Leverage is the use of debt to increase the earnings of the company. The company borrows $100 million at 7% and puts that money to work, where it earns 12%. This means that it is earning 5% in excess of its capital costs. The result is that $5 million is brought to the bottom line, which increases earnings and return on equity.

The problem with leverage is that it can make the company appear to have some kind of competitive advantage, when it in fact is just using large amounts of debt. Wall Street investment banks are notorious for the use of very large amounts of leverage to generate earnings. In their case they borrow $100 billion at, let us say, 6% and then loan it out at 7%, which means that they are earning 1% on the $100 billion, which equates to $1 billion. If that $1 billion shows up year after year, it creates the appearance of some kind of durable competitive advantage, even if there isn't one.

The problem is that while it appears that the investment bank has consistency in its income stream, the actual source that is sending it the interest payments may not be able to maintain the payments. This happened in the recent subprime-lending crisis that cost the banks hundreds of billions of dollars. They borrowed billions at, say, 6% and loaned it out at 8% to subprime homebuyers, which made them a ton of money. But when the economy started to slip, the subprime homebuyers started to default on their mortgages, which meant they stopped making interest payments. These subprime borrowers did not have a durable source of income, which ultimately meant that the investment banks didn't either.

In assessing the quality and durability of a company's competitive advantage, Warren has learned to avoid businesses that use a lot of leverage to help them generate earnings. In the short run they appear to be the goose that lays the golden eggs, but at the end of the day, they are not.

THE CASH FLOW
STATEMENT

*"There is a huge difference between the business that
grows and requires lots of capital to do so and the
business that grows and doesn't require capital."*

—WARREN BUFFETT

CHAPTER 50

The Cash Flow Statement:
Where Warren Goes to
Find the Cash

Most companies use what is called an Accrual Method of accounting, as opposed to a Cash Method. With the Accrual Method sales are booked when the goods go out the door, even if the buyer takes years to pay for them. With a Cash Method sales are only booked when the cash comes in. Because almost all businesses extend some kind of credit to their buyers, companies have found it more advantageous to use the Accrual Method, which allows them to book the sales on credit as income under accounts receivable on the income statement.

Since the Accrual Method of accounting allows credit sales to be booked as revenue it has become necessary for companies to keep separate track of the actual cash that flows in and out of the business. To this end, accountants created the cash flow statement.

A company can have a lot of cash coming in through the sale of shares or bonds and still not be profitable. (Similarly, a company can be profitable with a lot of sales on credit and not a lot of cash coming in.) The cash flow statement will tell us only if the company is bringing in more cash than it is spending ("positive cash flow") or if it is spending more cash than it is bringing in ("negative cash flow").

Cash flow statements are like income statements in that they always cover a set period of time. Company accountants generate one every three months and for the fiscal year.

The cash flow statement breaks down into three sections:

First, there is cash flow from operating activities: This area starts with net income and then adds back in depreciation and amortization. Though these are real expenses from an accounting point of view, they don't eat up any cash, because they represent cash that was eaten up years ago. What we end up with is Total Cash from Operating Activities.

($ in millions)	
Net Income	$5,981
Depreciation	1,163
Amortization	125
Total Cash from Operating Activities	$7,269

Next is cash flow from investing operations: This area includes an entry for all capital expenditures made for that accounting period. Capital expenditures is always a negative number because it's an expenditure, which causes a depletion of cash.

Also included in this category is Total Other Investing Cash Flow Items, which adds up all the cash that gets expended and brought in from the buying and selling of income-producing assets. If more cash is expended than is brought in, it is a negative number. If more cash is brought in than is expended, it is a positive number.

Both of these entries are added together to give us Total Cash from Investing Activities.

($ in millions)	
Capital Expenditures	($1,648)
Other Investing Cash Flow Items	(5,071)
Total Cash from Investing Activities	($6,719)

Finally, there is the section on cash flow from financing activities: This measures the cash that flows in and out of a company because of financing activities. This includes all outflows of cash for the payment of dividends. It also includes the selling and buying of the company's stock. When the company sells shares to finance a new plant, cash flows in to the company. When the company buys back its shares, cash flows out of the company. The same thing happens with bonds: Sell a bond and cash flows in; buy back a bond and cash flows out. All three of these entries are then added together to provide Total Cash from Financing Activities.

($ in millions)	
Cash Dividends Paid	($3,149)
Issuance (Retirement) of Stock, Net	(219)
Issuance (Retirement) of Debt, Net	4,341
Total Cash from Financing Activities	$973

Now if we add the Total Cash from Operating Activities, with Cash for Investing Activities, together with the Total Cash from Financing Activities, we get the company's Net Change in Cash.

($ in millions)	
Total Cash from Operating Activities	$7,269
Total Cash from Investing Activities	(6,719)
Total Cash from Financing Activities	973
Net Change in Cash	$1,523

What Warren has discovered is that some of the information found on a company's cash flow statement can be very useful in helping us determine whether or not the company in question is benefiting from having a durable competitive advantage. So let's roll up our sleeves and dive into the cash flow statement to see what Warren is seeing, as he searches for the company that will make him his next billion.

CHAPTER 51

CAPITAL EXPENDITURES:
NOT HAVING THEM IS ONE OF THE
SECRETS TO GETTING RICH

Cash Flow Statement	
($ in millions)	
→ Capital Expenditures	($1,648)
Other Investing Cash Flow Items	(5,071)
Total Cash from Investing Activities	($6,719)

Capital expenditures are outlays of cash or the equivalent in assets that are more permanent in nature—held longer than a year—such as property, plant, and equipment. They also include expenditures for such intangibles as patents. Basically they are assets that are expensed over a period of time greater than a year through depreciation or amortization. Capital expenditures are recorded on the cash flow statement under investment operations.

Buying a new truck for your company is a capital expenditure, the value of the truck will be expensed through depreciation over its life—let's say six years. But the gasoline used in the truck is a current expense, with the full price deducted from income during the current year.

When it comes to making capital expenditures, not all companies are created equal. Many companies must make huge capital expenditures just to stay in business. If capital expenditures remain high over a number of years, they can start to have deep impact on earnings. Warren has said that this is the reason that he never invested in telephone companies—the tremendous capital outlays in building out communication networks greatly hamper their long-term economics.

As a rule, a company with a durable competitive advantage uses a smaller portion of its earnings for capital expenditures for continuing operations than do those without a competitive advantage. Let's look at a couple of examples.

Coca-Cola, a long-time Warren favorite, over the last ten years earned a total $20.21 per share while only using $4.01 per share, or 19% of its total earnings, for capital expenditures for the same time period. Moody's, a company Warren has identified as having a durable competitive advantage, earned $14.24 a share over the last ten years while using a minuscule $0.84 a share, or 5% of its total earnings, for capital expenditures.

Compare Coke and Moody's with GM, which over the last ten years earned a total $31.64 a share after subtracting losses, while burning through a whopping $140.42 a share in capital expenditures. Or tiremaker Goodyear, which over the last ten years earned a total of $3.67 a share after subtracting losses and had total capital expenditures of $34.88 a share.

If GM used 444% more for capital expenditures than it earned, and Goodyear used 950%, where did all that extra money come from? It came from bank loans and from selling tons of new debt to the public. Such actions add more debt to these companies' balance sheets, which increases the amount of money they spend on interest payments, which is never a good thing.

Both Coke and Moody's, however, have enough excess income to have stock buyback programs that reduce the number of shares outstanding, while at the same time either reducing long-term debt or keeping it low. Both actions are big positives to Warren, and both helped him identify Coca-Cola and Moody's as businesses with a durable competitive advantage working in their favor.

When we look at capital expenditures in relation to net earnings we simply add up a company's total capital expenditures for a ten-year period and compare the figure with the company's total net earnings for the same ten-year period. The reason we look at a ten-year period is that it gives us a really good long-term perspective as to what is going on with the business.

Historically, durable competitive advantage companies used a far smaller percentage of their net income for capital expenditures. For instance, Wrigley annually uses approximately 49% of its net earnings for capital expenditures. Altria uses approximately 20%; Procter & Gamble, 28%; Pepsico, 36%; American Express, 23%; Coca-Cola, 19%; and Moody's, 5%.

Warren has discovered that if a company is historically using 50% or less of its annual net earnings for capital expenditures, it is a good place to look for a durable competitive advantage. If it is consistently using less than 25% of its net earnings for capital expenditures, that scenario occurs more than likely because the company has a durable competitive advantage working in its favor.

And having a durable competitive advantage working in our favor is what it is all about.

CHAPTER 52

STOCK BUYBACKS:
WARREN'S TAX-FREE WAY TO INCREASE
SHAREHOLDER WEALTH

Cash Flow Statement

Financing Cash Flow Items

($ in millions)

Total Cash Dividends Paid	($3,149)
→ Issuance (Retirement) of Stock, Net	(219)
Issuance (Retirement) of Debt, Net	4,341
Cash from Financing Activities	$973

In the above cash flow statement the company being examined paid out dividends of $3.149 million, bought back $219 million of its shares, and sold $4.341 million of new debt. All of this gave the company a net addition of $973 million in cash from financing activities.

Companies that have durable competitive advantage working in their favor make a ton of money, which creates the lovely problem of having to do something with it. If they don't just want to sit on it, or they can't reinvest it in the existing business or find a new business to invest in, they can either pay it out as dividends to their shareholders or use it to buy back shares. Since shareholders have to pay income tax on the dividends, Warren has never been too fond of using dividends to increase shareholders' wealth. This doesn't make anyone happy. A neater trick that Warren loves is to use some of the excess money that the company is throwing off to buy back the company's shares. This reduces the number of outstanding shares—which increases the remaining shareholders' interest in the company—and increases the per-share earnings of the company, which eventually makes the stock price go up.

Let's look at an example: If the company earned $10 million and has one million shares outstanding, it would have earnings of $10 a share. If we increase the number of shares outstanding to two million, the per-share earnings will drop to $5 a share. Likewise, if we decrease the number of shares outstanding to 500,000, we will increase the per-share earnings to $20 a share. More shares outstanding means lower per-share earnings, and lower shares outstanding means higher per-share earnings. Thus if the company buys back its own shares it can increase its per-share earnings figure even though actual net earnings don't increase. The best part is that there is an increase in the shareholders' wealth that they don't have to pay taxes on until they sell their stock. Think of it as the gift that keeps on giving.

Warren is such a big fan of this bit of financial engineering that he pushes the board of directors of all the excellent companies he invests in to buy back shares instead of increasing the dividend. He used it with GEICO, and he still is using it with The Washington Post Company.

To find out if a company is buying back its shares, go to the cash flow statement and look under Cash from Investing Activities. There you will find a heading titled "Issuance (Retirement) of Stock, Net." This entry nets out the selling and buying back of the company's shares. If the company is buying back its shares year after year, it is a good bet that it is a durable competitive advantage that is generating all the extra cash that allows it to do so.

In other words, one of the indicators of the presence of a durable competitive advantage is a "history" of the company repurchasing or retiring its shares.

VALUING THE COMPANY WITH A DURABLE COMPETITIVE ADVANTAGE

"I look for businesses in which I think I can predict what they're going to look like in ten to fifteen years' time. Take Wrigley's chewing gum. I don't think the Internet is going to change how people chew gum."

—WARREN BUFFETT

CHAPTER 53

WARREN'S REVOLUTIONARY IDEA
OF THE EQUITY BOND AND HOW IT HAS
MADE HIM SUPERRICH

In the late 1980s, Warren gave a talk at Columbia University about how companies with a durable competitive advantage show such great strength and predictability in earnings growth that growth turns their shares into a kind of equity bond, with an ever-increasing coupon or interest payment. The "bond" is the company's shares/equity, and the "coupon/interest payment" is the company's pretax earnings. Not the dividends that the company pays out, but the actual pretax earnings of the business.

This is how Warren buys an entire business: He looks at its pretax earnings and asks if the purchase is a good deal relative to the economic strength of the company's underlying economics and the price being asked for the business. He uses the same reasoning when he is buying a partial interest in a company via the stock market.

What attracts Warren to the conceptual conversion of a company's shares into equity/bonds is that the durable competitive advantage of the business creates underlying economics that are so strong they cause a continuing increase in the company's earnings. With this increase in earnings comes an eventual increase in the price of the company's shares as the stock market acknowledges the increase in the underlying value of the company.

Thus, at the risk of being repetitive, to Warren the shares of a company with a durable competitive advantage are the equivalent of equity/bonds, and the company's pretax earnings are the equivalent of a normal bond's coupon or interest payment. But instead of the bond's coupon or interest rate being fixed, it keeps increasing year after year, which naturally increases the equity/bond's value year after year.

This is what happens when Warren buys into a company with a durable competitive advantage. The per-share earnings continue to rise over time—either through increased business, expansion of operations, the purchase of new businesses, or the repurchase of shares with money that accumulates in the company's coffers. With the rise in earnings comes a corresponding increase in the return that Warren is getting on his original investment in the equity bond.

Let's look at an example to see how his theory works.

In the late 1980s, Warren started buying shares in Coca-Cola for an average price of $6.50 a share against pretax earnings of $.70 a share, which equates to after-tax earnings of

$.46 a share. Historically, Coca-Cola's earnings had been growing at an annual rate of around 15%. Seeing this, Warren could argue that he just bought a Coca-Cola equity bond that is paying an initial pretax interest rate of 10.7% on his $6.50 investment. He could also argue that that yield would increase over time at a projected annual rate of 15%.

Understand that, unlike the Graham-based value investors, Warren is not saying that Coca-Cola is worth $60 and is trading at $40 a share; therefore it is "undervalued." What he is saying is that at $6.50 a share, he was being offered a relatively risk-free initial pretax rate of return of 10.7%, which he expected to increase over the next twenty years at an annual rate of approximately 15%. Then he asked himself if that was an attractive investment given the rate of risk and return on other investments.

To the Graham-based value investors, a pretax 10.7% rate of return growing at 15% a year would not be interesting since they are only interested in the stock's market price and, regardless of what happens to the business, have no intention of holding the investment for more than a couple of years. But to Warren, who plans on owning the equity bond for twenty or more years, it is his dream investment.

Why is it his dream investment? Because with each year that passes, his return on his initial investment actually increases, and in the later years the numbers really start to pyramid. Consider this: Warren's initial investment in The Washington Post Company cost him $6.36 a share. Thirty-four years later, in 2007, the media company is earning a pretax $54 a share, which equates to an after-tax return of $34 a share. This gives Warren's Washington Post equity bonds a current pretax yield of 849%, which equates to an after-tax yield of 534%. (And you were wondering how Warren got so rich!)

So how did Warren do with his Coca-Cola equity bonds?

By 2007 Coca-Cola's pretax earnings had grown at an annual rate of approximately 9.35% to $3.96 a share, which equates to an after-tax $2.57 a share. This means that Warren can argue that his Coke equity bonds are now paying him a pretax return of $3.96 a share on his original investment of $6.50 a share, which equates to a current pretax yield of 60% and a current after-tax yield of 40%.

The stock market, seeing this return, over time, will eventually revalue Warren's equity bonds to reflect this increase in value.

Consider this: With long-term corporate interest rates at approximately 6.5% in 2007, Warren's Washington Post equity bonds/shares, with a pretax $54 earnings/interest payment, were worth approximately $830 per equity bond/share that year ($54 ÷ .065 = $830). During 2007, Warren's Washington Post equity bonds/shares traded in a range of between $726 and $885 a share, which is right about in line with the equity bond's capitalized value of $830 a share.

We can witness the same stock market revaluing phenomenon with Warren's Coca-Cola equity bonds. In 2007 they earned a pretax $3.96 per equity bond/share, which equates to an after-tax $2.57 per equity bond/share. Capitalized at the corporate interest rate of 6.5%, Coke's pretax earnings of $3.96 are worth approximately $60 per equity bond/share ($3.96 ÷ .065 = $60). During 2007, the stock market valued Coca-Cola between $45 and $64 a share.

One of the reasons that the stock market eventually tracks the increase in these companies' underlying values is that their earnings are so consistent, they are an open invitation to a leveraged buyout. If a company carries little debt and has a strong earnings history, and its stock price falls low enough, another company will come in and buy it, financing the purchase with the acquired company's earnings. Thus when interest rates drop, the company's earnings are worth more, because they will support more debt, which makes the company's shares worth more. And when interest rates rise, the earnings are worth less, because they will support less debt. This makes the company's stock worth less.

What Warren has learned is that if he buys a company with a durable competitive advantage, the stock market, over time, will price the company's equity bonds/shares at a level that reflects the value of its earnings relative to the yield on long-term corporate bonds. Yes, some days the stock market is pessimistic and on others is full of wild optimism, but in the end it is long-term interest rates that determine the economic reality of what long-term investments are worth.

CHAPTER 54

THE EVER-INCREASING YIELD
CREATED BY THE DURABLE
COMPETITIVE ADVANTAGE

To belabor the point, because it is definitely worth belaboring, let's look at a couple of Warren's other favorite durable competitive advantage companies to see if the yields on their equity bonds/shares have increased over time:

In 1998 Moody's' reported after-tax earnings of $.41 per share. By 2007 Moody's after-tax earnings had grown to $2.58 a share. Warren paid $10.38 a share for his Moody's equity bonds, and today they are earning an after-tax yield of 24%, which equates to a pretax yield of 38%.

In 1998 American Express had after-tax earnings of $1.54 a share. By 2008 its after-tax earnings had increased to $3.39 a share. Warren paid $8.48 a share for his American Express equity bonds, which means they are currently yielding an after-tax 40% rate of return, which equates to a 61% pretax rate of return.

Long-time Warren favorite Procter & Gamble earned an after-tax $1.28 a share in 1998. By 2007 it had after-tax earnings of $3.31 a share. Warren paid $10.15 a share for his Procter & Gamble equity bonds, which are now yielding an after-tax 32%, which equates to a pretax return of 49%.

With See's Candy Warren bought the whole company for $25 million back in 1972. In 2007 it had pretax earnings of $82 million, which means his See's equity bonds are now producing an annual pretax yield of 328% on his original investment.

With all these companies, their durable competitive advantage caused their earnings to increase year after year, which, in turn, increased the underlying value of the business. Yes, the stock market may take its own sweet time acknowledging this increase, but it will eventually happen, and Warren has banked on that "happening" many, many times.

CHAPTER 55

More Ways to Value a Company with a Durable Competitive Advantage

As stated earlier, in 1987 Warren started buying shares in Coca-Cola for an average price of $6.50 a share against pretax earnings of $.70 a share; this equates to after-tax earnings of $.46 a share. Historically, Coca-Cola's earnings had been growing at an annual rate of around 10%.

Seeing this, Warren could argue that he had just bought a Coca-Cola equity bond paying an initial pretax interest rate of 10.7% on his $6.50 investment. He could also argue that that pretax yield would increase over time at a projected annual rate of 10% (Coca-Cola's average annual rate of earnings growth for the ten years prior to 1987).

If, in 1987, he had projected out the earnings growth of 10% forward, he could have argued that by 2007 Coca-Cola would have pretax per-share earnings of $4.35 and after-tax earnings of $2.82 a share. This would mean that by 2007 his pretax return on his Coca-Cola equity bonds would grow to 66%, which equates to an after-tax return of 43%.

So what was a pretax 66% return on a $6.50 equity bond in 2007 worth in 1987? It depends on the discount rate that we use. If we use 7%, which is right about what long-term rates were back then, we get a discounted back value of approximately 17%. Multiply 17% by the $6.50 a share he was paying for and we would get $1.10 a share. Multiply $1.10 by Coca-Cola's 1987 P/E of 14 and we get $15.40 per share. Thus Warren could have argued in 1987 that he was buying an equity bond for $6.50 a share, and that if he held it for twenty years, its 1987 intrinsic value really would be $15.40 a share.

By 2007 Coca-Cola's pretax earnings had grown at an annual rate of 9.35% to $3.96 a share, which equates to an after-tax $2.57 a share. This means that Warren can argue that his Coca-Cola equity bonds are now paying him a pretax return of $3.96 a share on his original investment of $6.50 a share, which equates to a current pretax yield of 60% and an after-tax yield of 40%.

The stock market in 2007 valued Warren's equity bonds at between $45 and $64 a share. In 2007 Coca-Cola earned a pretax $3.96 per equity bond/share, which equated to an after-tax $2.57 per equity bond/share. Capitalized at the 2007 corporate interest rate of 6.5%, Coca-Cola's pretax earnings of $3.96 a share are worth approximately $60 per equity bond/share ($3.96 ÷ .065 = $60). This is in line with the 2007 stock market value at between $45 and $64 a share.

With the market valuing Warren's Coca-Cola equity bonds at $64 a share in 2007, Warren could calculate that he has been earning a tax-deferred annual compounding rate of return of 12.11% on his original investment. Think of it as a bond that paid an annual rate of return of 12.11% without tax on the interest earned. Not only that: You got to reinvest all those interest payments in more bonds that were paying 12.11%. Yes, someday you will have to pay taxes when you sell your equity bonds, but if you don't sell them you just keep on earning 12.11% free of taxes year after year after year. . . .

Don't believe it? Consider this: Warren has approximately $64 billion in capital gains on his Berkshire stock and has yet to pay a penny in taxes on it. The greatest accumulation of private wealth in the history of the world and not a penny paid to the taxman.

Does it get any better?

CHAPTER 56

HOW WARREN DETERMINES THE RIGHT
TIME TO BUY A FANTASTIC BUSINESS

In Warren's world the price you pay directly affects the return on your investment. Since he is looking at a company with a durable competitive advantage as being a kind of equity bond, the higher the price he pays, the lower his initial rate of return and the lower the rate of return on the company's earnings in ten years. Let's look at an example: In the late 1980s, Warren started buying Coca-Cola for an average price of $6.50 a share against earnings of a $.46 a share, which in Warren's world equates to an initial rate of return of 7%. By 2007 Coca-Cola was earning $2.57 a share. This means that Warren can argue that his Coca-Cola equity bond was now paying him $2.57 a share on his original investment of $6.50, which equates to a return of 39.9%. But if he had paid $21 a share for his Coca-Cola stock back in the late 1980s, his initial rate of return would have been 2.2%. By 2007 this would have grown only to

12% ($2.57 ÷ $21 = 12%), which is definitely not as attractive a number as 39.9%.

Thus the lower the price you pay for a company with a durable competitive advantage, the better you are going to do over the long-term, and Warren is all about the long-term. However, these companies seldom, if ever, sell at a bargain price from an old-school Grahamian perspective. This is why investment managers who follow the value doctrine that Graham preached never own super businesses, because to them these businesses are too expensive.

So when do you buy in to them? In bear markets for starters. Though they might still seem high priced compared with other "bear market bargains," in the long run they are actually the better deal. And occasionally even a company with a durable competitive advantage can screw up and do something stupid, which will send its stock price downward over the short-term. Think New Coke. Warren has said that a wonderful buying opportunity can present itself when a great business confronts a one-time solvable problem. The key here is that the problem is solvable.

When do you want to stay away from these super businesses? At the height of bull markets, when these super businesses trade at historically high price-to-earnings ratios. Even a company that benefits from having a durable competitive advantage can't unmoor itself from producing mediocre results for investors if they pay too steep a price for admission.

CHAPTER 57

How Warren Determines It Is
Time to Sell

In Warren's world you would never sell one of these wonderful businesses as long as it maintained its durable competitive
advantage. The simple reason is that the longer you hold on
to them, the better you do. Also, if at any time you sold one
these great investments, you would be inviting the taxman to
the party. Inviting the taxman to your party too many times
makes it very hard to get superrich. Consider this: Warren's
company has about $36 billion in capital gains from his
investments in companies that have durable competitive
advantages. This is wealth he hasn't yet paid a dime of tax on,
and if he has it his way, he never will.

Still, there are times that it is advantageous to sell one of
these wonderful businesses. The first is when you need money
to make an investment in an even better company at a better
price, which occasionally happens.

The second is when the company looks like it is going to

lose its durable competitive advantage. This happens periodically, as with newspapers and television stations. Both of them used to be fantastic businesses. But the Internet came along and suddenly the durability of their competitive advantage was called into question. A questionable competitive advantage is not where you want to keep your money long-term.

The third is during bull markets when the stock market, in an insane buying frenzy, sends the prices on these fantastic businesses through the ceiling. In these cases, the current selling price of the company's stock far exceeds the long-term economic realities of the business. And the long-term economic realities of a business are like gravity when stock prices climb up into the outer limits. Eventually they will pull the stock price back down to earth. If they climb too high, the economics of selling and putting the proceeds into another investment may outweigh the benefits afforded by continued ownership of the business. Think of it this way: If we can project that the business we own will earn $10 million over the next twenty years, and someone today offers us $5 million for the entire company, do we take it? If we can only invest the $5 million at a 2% annual compounding rate of return, probably not, since the $5 million invested today at a 2% compounding annual rate of return would be worth only $7.4 million by year twenty. Not a great deal for us. But if we could get an annual compounding rate of return of 8%, our $5 million would have grown to $23 million by year twenty. Suddenly, selling out looks like a real sweet deal.

A simple rule is that when we see P/E ratios of 40 or more on these super companies, and it does occasionally happen, it just might be time to sell. But if we do sell into a raging bull market, then we shouldn't go out and buy something else trading at 40 times earnings. Instead, we should take a break, put our money into U.S. Treasuries and wait for the next bear market. Because there is always another bear market right around the corner, just waiting to give us the golden opportunity to buy into one or more of these amazing durable competitive advantage businesses that will, over the long-term, make us super superrich.

Just like Warren Buffett.

APPENDIX

Model Balance Sheet of a Company with a Durable Competitive Advantage

($ in millions)

Assets

Cash & Short-Term Investments	$4,208
Total Inventory	2,220
Total Receivables, Net	3,317
Prepaid Expenses	2,260
Other Current Assets, Total	0
Total Current Assets	12,005
Property/Plant/Equipment	8,493
Goodwill, Net	4,246
Intangibles, Net	7,863
Long-Term Investments	7,777
Other Long-Term Assets	2,675
Other Assets	0
Total Assets	$43,059

Liabilities

Accounts Payable	$1,380
Accrued Expenses	5,535
Short-Term Debt	5,919
Long-Term Debt Due	133
Other Current Liabilities	258
Total Current Liabilities	13,225
Long-Term Debt	3,277
Deferred Income Tax	1,890
Minority Interest	0
Other Liabilities	3,133
Total Liabilities	$21,525

Shareholders' Equity

Preferred Stock	0
Common Stock	880
Additional Paid in Capital	7,378
Retained Earnings	36,235
Treasury Stock, Common	−23,375
Other Equity	626
Total Shareholders' Equity	21,744
Total Liabilities & Shareholders' Equity	$43,269

Model Balance Sheet of a Mediocre Company
without a Durable Competitive Advantage

($ in millions)

Assets

Cash & Short-Term Investments	$28,000
Total Inventory	10,190
Total Receivables, Net	69,787
Prepaid Expenses	260
Other Current Assets, Total	5
Total Current Assets	108,242
Property/Plant/Equipment	40,012
Goodwill, Net	736
Intangibles, Net	333
Long-Term Investments	43,778
Other Long-Term Assets	22,675
Other Assets	5,076
Total Assets	$220,852

Liabilities

Accounts Payable	$22,468
Accrued Expenses	5,758
Short-Term Debt	32,919
Long-Term Debt Due	920
Other Current Liabilities	258
Total Current Liabilities	62,323
Long-Term Debt	133,277
Deferred Income Tax	5,890
Minority Interest	0
Other Liabilities	3,133
Total Liabilities	$204,623

Shareholders' Equity

Preferred Stock	$150
Common Stock	880
Additional Paid in Capital	7,378
Retained Earnings	8,235
Treasury Stock, Common	0
Other Equity	−414
Total Shareholders' Equity	16,229
Total Liabilities & Shareholders' Equity	$220,852

Model Income Statement of a Company with a Durable Competitive Advantage

($ in millions)

Revenue	$28,857
Cost of Goods Sold	10,406
Gross Profit	18,451
Operating Expenses	
Selling, General & Administration	10,200
Research & Development	0
Depreciation	1,107
Operating Profit	7,144
Interest Expense	456
Gain (Loss) Sale Assets	1,275
Other	50
Income Before Tax	7,913
Income Taxes Paid	2,769
Net Earnings	$5,144

Model Income Statement of a Company
without a Durable Competitive Advantage

($ in millions)

Revenue	$172,455
Cost of Goods Sold	142,587
Gross Profit	29,868
Operating Expenses	
Selling, General & Administration	20,170
Research & Development	5,020
Depreciation	6,800
Operating Profit (Loss)	(2,122)
Interest Expense	10,200
Gain (Loss) Sale Assets	402
Other	35
Income Before Tax (Loss)	(11,955)
Income Taxes Paid	0
Net Earnings	($11,955)

Select Glossary of Terms

AAA rating: The highest rating that Standard & Poor's gives to a company for its financial soundness.

It doesn't get any better than this. The company is golden if it gets this rating.

accounts receivable: Money owed to the company for goods sold that haven't been paid for yet.

Having lots of accounts receivable is a good thing, but having lots of cash is even better.

accumulated depreciation: The total of all depreciation, or decreases in value, that has been charged against an asset.

Accountants like to keep track of everything, including how much things depreciate. Think of accumulated depreciation as a very large trash can you can check to find how much the company's assets have depreciated.

amortization: Basically, the same as depreciation, but it applies to intangible assets such as goodwill and patents.

Depreciation applies to tangible assets such as a manufacturing plant. The problem with patents, for example, is that they don't really depreciate, so the cost of the patent is spread out (amortized) over a number of years as a cost.

asset: Something that is owned by the business and is expected to be used to generate future income.

Having lots of assets is a good thing. Having lots of assets that produce lots of money is an even better thing.

balance sheet: A summary of a company's assets, liabilities, and ownership equity as of a specific date, such as the end of its fiscal year.

A balance sheet is often described as a snapshot of a company's financial condition on a single day within the year. There is no such thing as a balance sheet for a longer period of time. A balance sheet tells you how much you have and how much you owe. Subtract one from the other and you get how much you are worth.

bond: A security that represents long-term debt.

Companies with durable competitive advantages don't have a lot of bonds because they usually don't have a lot of debt. And not having a lot of debt is a good thing.

book value: All of the company's assets minus all of the company's liabilities. Divide this by the number of common shares outstanding, and you get the per-share book value of the company.

Increasing book value is a good thing; decreasing book value is a bad thing.

capital expenditures: The amount the company spends every year on building new or upgrading old infrastructure.

Companies with a durable competitive advantage tend to have low capital expenditures.

cash flow: The amount of cash generated by the company during a specific period. Cash flow for a company is tracked on the cash flow statement.

common stock: Securities that represent ownership in the business. Holders of common stock are entitled to elect a board of directors, receive dividends, and collect all the proceeds from the sale of a company after all of its debts have been paid.

Warren got rich by buying the common stock of companies.

competitive advantage: An edge over competitors that allows the company to make more money.

The more cash a company can generate, the happier its shareholders. Warren is only interested in companies that have a competitive advantage that can be maintained over a long period of time.

cost of goods sold: The cost of inventory sold during a specific period. Or the cost of obtaining raw goods and making finished products.

Low cost of goods sold relative to revenue is a good thing; high costs are a bad thing.

current assets: Assets—*things of value*—that are cash or are expected to be converted into cash within a year. These assets are found on the balance sheet and include cash, cash equivalents, accounts receivable, inventory, and prepaid expenses.

current liabilities: Money owed within a year.

current ratio: The ratio of current assets to current liabilities.

Current ratio is of little use in the search for the company with a durable competitive advantage.

depreciation: Tangible assets wear out as they are used. As they wear out, a depreciation charge is taken against the asset.

durable competitive advantage: A competitive advantage over a company's competitors that it can maintain for a long period of time.

This is the secret to Warren's success and the reason that you are reading this book.

EBITDA: Earnings before interest, taxes, depreciation, and amortization.

Companies that don't make money love EBITDA. Warren thinks that EBITDA is stupid. Whenever you hear management talking in terms of EBITDA, it means that they don't have a durable competitive advantage.

financial statement: The balance sheet, income statement, and cash flow statement.

This shows where all the goodies are kept, but you need to see them from a number of years if you really want to tell what is going on.

goodwill: The value of an asset in excess of the value that is carried on the books.

The company has a per-share book value of $10 and a selling price of $15 a share. The $5 in excess of the book value is booked as goodwill if the company was bought by another company.

gross margin: The ratio of total profit to sales.

The higher the better. Companies with a durable competitive advantage tend to have high gross margins.

gross profit: Proceeds on product sales. Sales minus cost of goods sold equals gross profit.

It's good to bounce other numbers off the gross profit.

income statement: The statement that shows a company's income and expenses for a specific period.

A single year's income statement tells us very little. We need to check out five-to-ten years' worth of income statements if we are really serious about finding out if the company has a durable competitive advantage.

intangible assets: Assets such as patents and copyrights, which can't be physically touched, but can generate income.

Think of these as monopolies protected by law, which is a

kind of durable competitive advantage. The only problem with patents is that they eventually expire, or lose their protection. When this happens, any and every company in the world can produce the product and the company loses the competitive advantage the patent once provided. This is the reason why Warren has historically stayed away from the drug manufacturers.

interest expense: The amount of money a company pays in interest on both its long- and short-term debt.

Companies without a durable competitive advantage tend to have a lot of interest expense because they have a lot of debt. Companies with a durable competitive advantage tend not to have any debt so they have little or no interest expense.

inventory: A company's products that are either completed or in some stage of completion and that will be sold to the company's customers.

If sales are decreasing and inventory is rising, watch out.

leverage: The amount of debt the company has in relation to the shareholders' equity.

The presence of a large amount of leverage over a long period of time usually means that the company doesn't have a durable competitive advantage.

liabilities: The obligations the company has to pay others.

Liabilities are listed on the company's balance sheet. They are not a good thing to have. A company should strive to have as few as possible.

long-term debt: Debt that has a maturity date of longer than one year.

Companies with a durable competitive advantage tend to have little or no long-term debt.

mediocre business: A company that doesn't have a durable competitive advantage and suffers the intense pressures of competition.

This is the kind of company that will make you poor over the long run.

net income: The company's profit after all costs, expenses, and taxes are deducted from revenue.

The more net income, the better. The more consistent the net income, the more likely the company has a durable competitive advantage.

operating expenses: Costs of running the business that are not tied directly to the production costs of the company's products.

Lower is better.

operating profit: The company's earnings from ongoing operations. This is equal to earnings before deductions for interest payments and income taxes. Also called EBIT (earnings before interest and taxes) or operating income.

outstanding shares: Common stock held by investors. Does not include treasury shares, but does include restricted shares owned by corporate officers and insiders.

A dramatic increase in the number of shares outstanding over a number of years without an increase in the company's earnings usually means that the company is selling new shares to increase its capital base to make up for the fact that it is a mediocre business. Warren stays away from mediocre businesses.

preferred stock: Capital stock that provides a specific dividend and grants no voting rights.

Companies with a durable competitive advantage tend not to have any preferred stock.

prepaid expense: A current asset that represents an expense that was paid before or at the beginning of the accounting period in which the benefit of the expense will be received.

research and development expense: The amount of money a company spends in a given period of time on producing and improving new products.

Companies with a durable competitive advantage tend to have little or no research and development expenses.

retained earnings: Accumulated net earnings of the business that have not been paid out as a dividend.

A solid long-term growth in retained earnings is one of the marks of a company with a durable competitive advantage.

return on equity: A company's net income divided by its shareholders' equity.

This is one of the ways that Warren tells if the company has a durable competitive advantage. The higher the better.

revenues: Money received or that is due from the sale of the company's products or services.

Revenue is where it all starts, but it should never be used as the only way to value a business, unless you work on Wall Street and are trying to sell the public on a company that doesn't earn any money.

SGA costs: Selling, general, and administrative expenses, which report the company's costs for direct and indirect selling expenses and all general and administrative expenses that were incurred during the accounting period. This includes management salaries, advertising, travel costs, legal fees, commissions, all payroll costs, and the like.

Lower is better.

shareholders' equity: The net worth of the business. Total assets minus total liabilities equals shareholders' equity.

treasury shares: What is known as treasury stock in the United States is referred to as treasury shares in the United Kingdom.

treasury stock: The company's common stock that has been repurchased by the company. Treasury stock grants no voting rights or the right to receive dividends and should not be included in the outstanding shares calculations.

Having treasury stock tells us that the company just might have a durable competitive advantage.

undervalued company: A company that is selling in the stock market at a price below its long-term worth as a business.

Benjamin Graham bought undervalued companies and made millions. Warren bought companies with a durable competitive advantage and made billions.

Acknowlwedgments

We owe a great debt to Warren Buffett for his kindness, generosity, and wisdom over the years. If we thanked him a million times it would not be enough.

We also are thankful that Scribner is our publishing house. We specifically wish to thank our publishers Susan Moldow and Roz Lippel, who have given us a great deal of freedom in the writing of this book. We also owe a very special thank-you to Roz for those finishing touches that only a great editor can add. We also wish to thank Tom Dussel for his brilliant handling of our international partners who publish our books.

We also wish to thank our retired publisher Eleanor Rawson, who had the vision to publish our first book, *Buffettology*.

I, Mary, wish to dedicate this book to the most important people in my life, my family. First, my children, Erica, Nicole, and Sam, who give me the most love and happiness, making me prouder of them every day. My sisters, Dorothy Manley, for always being there for me through thick and thin, and Laura Sir Mons, whom I still look to for the very important part of life, living it to the fullest. Jim Manley, my brother-in-law, who always inspires us to reach perfection by practice practice practice. . . .

I also wish to thank "Just" Joe Campbell, the kindest person I know and love; Jocelyn Skinner, my best friend, who keeps my world spinning; the amazing Richard Bangs, adventurer and true friend; Scott Daggatt, for his friendship and counsel extraordinaire; Rita Watnick and Michael Stoyla, for always believing in me and helping me at every turn; my new friend and brilliant mind Bob McElwee; the miraculous Debbie Levin for her friendship and the important work she does as president of the Environmental Media Association; Ken Spratford, my 911 "Buddy"; and Janos Kalla, for keeping me sane and for always being there. I also wish to thank Jay Hill, my co-blogger and the smartest girl I know. And a very special thank-you to the great musician/composer Ken Hankins, aka "Joy," who inspires me every day.

David wishes to thank Kate and Dexter for all their love, Sam and Andy for being great brothers, and Cindy Connolly and Bob Eisenberg for being the fantastic friends that they always have been. He owes a special gratitude to artists Terry Rosenberg and Steve Joy for always answering the call to coffee and to filmmaker Alexander Payne for many really great conversations. He gives a special thank-you to Todd Simon for a ton of things, including bringing Betiana and Mia into our lives.

David also wishes to thank Wyoming attorney Gerry Spence for his deep friendship and helpful guidance over many years. No man ever had a better or more interesting friend.

And last, but not least, we both wish to thank the late Benjamin Graham, who planted the tree we all came to sit under.

INDEX

Page numbers in *italics* refer to tables.

total inventory, 70
total liabilities, 127
total other investing cash flow
    items, 149
total receivables, 70
trademarks, 96
travel costs, 39
Treasury bills, 78, 175
treasury shares, 189
treasury stock, 137, 138, 139,
    189–90

undervalued companies, 190
unique products, 12–13, 15
unique services, 13–14, 15
United Airlines:
    gross profit margin of, 34
    interest payments of, 51
    return on shareholders' equity
        of, 141
U.S. Steel, gross profit margin of, 34

value investing, xviii, 3, 6–7, 9, 98,
    163, 172
volatility, 98

wages payable, 108
Wal-Mart, 14
    brand name of, 97

Washington Post Company, 10,
    12
    as "equity bond," 163–64
    long-term debt of, 118
    stocks bought back by, 158
Washington Public Power Supply
    System (WPPSS), 56
Wells Fargo & Co., 13, 51
    competitive advantage of,
        111–12
    retained earnings of, 133
Wrigley:
    as brand name, 97
    capital expenditures of, 155
    debt to shareholders' equity ratio
        of, 124
    depreciation and, 48
    durable competitive advantage
        of, 91–92
    gross profit margin of, 33
    interest expenses of, 50
    long-term debt of, 118
    plant and equipment of, 91–92
    as predictable, 159
    return on shareholders' equity
        of, 141
    as unique, 12, 13

Yahoo!, 20, 21

About the Authors

Mary Buffett is an internationally best-selling author and speaker on the investment methods of Warren Buffett. David Clark is an internationally recognized authority on the subject of Buffettology and the managing partner of a private investment group in Omaha, Nebraska. Together, they have written four best-selling books on the investment methods of Warren Buffett. Their books, *The Tao of Warren Buffett, The New Buffettology, The Buffettology Workbook,* and *Buffettology,* have been published in more than seventeen languages worldwide, including Chinese, Russian, Hebrew, and Arabic.

For Continuing Education in Buffettology

For continuing education in the investment methods of Warren Buffett, please visit Buffettology Seminars' website at:

www.buffettologyseminars.com.

Or, contact Mary Buffett or David Clark directly at:

Marybuffettology@gmail.com or
Davidbuffettology@gmail.com.